© Copyright 2023 by Sandy Stanway – All rights reserved.

It is not legal to reproduce, duplicate, or transmit any part of this document in either electronic means or printed format. recording of this publication is strictly prohibited.

ISBN 978-0-473-69149-3

PLEASE NOTE:-

ALL IDEAS, SUGGESTIONS AND INCOME INDICATIONS PRESENTED IN THE FOLLOWING PAGES ARE THAT OF THE AUTHORS, BASED ON HER RESEARCH AND MEANT AS A GUIDELINE. PLEASE ENSURE YOU DO YOU OWN THOROUGH RESEARCH AND DUE DILIGENCE PRIOR TO UNDERTAKING ANY OF THE FOLLOWING IDEAS. PLEASE ALSO NOTE THAT COSTS AND FEES THAT CAN BE CHARGED MAY VARY FROM LOCATION TO LOCATION.

www.SandyStanway.com

50 Ways to Make Money Working With Horses

Adult Fun Horse Camps 5

Adult Riding Lessons 8

Animal Aunts/Holiday Accommodation for Horses 12

Breaking in horses or Starting them under saddle 15

Breed Horses to sell 19

Build and sell Obstacles and/or Show Jumps 23

Buying and Bringing On/Upskill 25

Buying and Selling Horse Feed and/or Hay 28

Buying horses for other people 31

Clinician giving Lessons, Clinics or Camps 34

Clipping 37

Competitions like Road to the Horse (USA), Kaimanawa Stallion Challenge (NZ), Thoroughbred OTTB Makeovers (Multiple Countries hold this) or the Extreme Mustang Makeover (USA) 39

Equine body worker/Chiropractor 43

Equine Show Turnout Services 45

Facility Hire – Arena, Jumps, Obstacles, a Gallop track or Cross Country Jumps 48

Fix and Flick ponies 51

Foaling Attendant..54

Foundation Training 56

Grazing/Boarding/Agistment/Livery Horse Services 59

Hoof Trimming 65

Horse Adventure Park	68
Horse Gear Hire/Lease/Hire horse Floats/trailers	72
Horse Trekking/Guided Rides	76
Hosting visiting Instructors/Clinicians	79
Judging	82
Kids Fun Pony Holiday Camps	84
Kids Riding Lessons	87
Make Horse Sales Videos	90
Nightshow Performances	92
Online Video Courses	94
Photographing Horses	97
Picking Up Manure	101
Pony Club (4H) Instructors – note this differs from being a Clinician (as generally this is for one on one lessons) and giving riding lessons (as you don't have to provide horses)	104
Pony Parties	106
Pre-School Training	110
Problem Solving	113
Retired Horse Sanctuary/Racehorse spelling	116
Sale on Behalf	119
Schooling – like bringing horses back into work or putting miles in the saddle	122
Sell Horse Manure – Liquid, Powered or Normal	125
Selling Horse Themed Giftware	128
Selling Specialised Equestrian Equipment	131
Show Preparation/Thoroughbred (TB) Yearling Sales Prep	134

Teaching a Specific Skill to a Horse 137
Thoroughbred Racehorse Breeding 139
Transporting Horses 143
Vet Assistant at an Equine Hospital 146
Virtual Lessons 148
Working on a Yard/Stable Groom 150
Young Horse Nursery 152

Adult Fun Horse Camps

WHAT IS IT?
These have become more popular in recent years. This is where you offer the opportunity for a group of adults to come to your facility or a place you hire, and then give them lessons, entertain, educate and generally amuse them for a number of days. The average length of an adult camp ranges from 3-5 days. These camps differ from a normal horsemanship type camp in that they generally have a range of topics covered e.g. playing with obstacles, saddle fit, teeth, swimming the horses, sometimes beach rides depending on the location of the camp etc as well demonstrations, entertainment and games (fun). These camps are normally live in and include meals. These have been really popular with recreational riders as well as those involved in competitions just looking for some time out. Numbers on these camps range from 10 – 30.

POTENTIAL INCOME
The average cost of the camps is around NZ$575 (GBP£276/US$342) per person x by 30 = NZ$17,250 (GBP£8,284/US$10,261) per camp less expenses. This is a good income but does require a drawcard to get the people there. This could be talk by a famous person or a special lesson with someone exciting. Our you could have a big enough client base to get this number of people along. It also requires the ability to accommodate and feed this number of people. So although this is very good income for a short period of time, it does have some logistical considerations. I know a number of venues that could cater for this number of people with the facilities to run a great camp, so if you look around I am sure you could find something similar. On these camps the adults normally bring their own horses.

Note again you need to make sure you have the correct public liability insurance in place to cover an event like this, because if someone does get hurt, you do not want to be facing a law suite or similar.

PRO'S
- This type of event can produce a significant amount of income
- You get to meet some very interesting people
- This type of camp can be great fun
- Anyone who has organised and run camps will find this reasonably easy to organise

CON'S
- There is a huge amount of work organising an event like this – venue, food, catering, program, lesson organisation (groups or individual), organising speakers if you are having speakers, planning and preparing demonstrations, first aid provisions, keeping a large number of horses and people engaged and happy for this length of time takes considerable skill and effort etc etc etc
- You need to have good facilities – Good facilities make running something like this a lot easier as you already have sufficient yards and accommodation so you are not trying to temporarily set up something and then having to take it all down after the event which is a lot more work. You have to be able to house/accommodate the number of horses and people involved
- You have to be able to structure a program that will keep everyone entertained and involved for the whole time

WHAT YOU NEED TO GET STARTED AND BE ABLE TO DO THIS
There are four main things required to get this type of event underway – suitable venue, insurances to cover any possible liability if someone gets hurt, enough suitably qualified instructors/leaders and enough

potential participants. Once you have found a suitable venue generating enough customers for the event to go ahead is the biggest difficulty but as stated above if you can find a draw card e.g. a talk from famous person, or a ride on your best horse or a great prize or something they can't get anywhere else then you stand a good chance of getting enough participants to make this a huge success.

Structuring a great program will also help. Ideally ensuring you include a combination of individual lessons, group lessons, demonstrations, talks, fun activities, playing with obstacles if you have them available (adults love playing with obstacles). Effectively a great combination of education and entertainment.

Adult Riding Lessons

WHAT IS IT?
There are two different types of adult riding lessons. The first is where you supply the horse for the adult to learn on and the second is where the adult student brings their own horse to you/or you go to the student and give them a lesson on their horse. Both types of lessons can be done individually or in a group.

Both of these types have pros and cons. Giving adults lessons on your horses means you are able to control the quality of the horse they ride, as well as where the lesson takes place and what you focus on.

Giving lessons on their horse is another matter entirely. When someone uses their own horse you have to have the skills to be able to help them with what they need help with. They may want to focus on dressage but their horse won't stand still to be mounted or they have problems saddling it up so you may have to focus on that. Their horse may have significant behavioural issues that require addressing like bucking, bolting or rearing that again require you to have the skills to be able to help student with. I have found a lot of people who are good at riding do not always make the best instructors/teachers. To be a great teacher you have to be able to communicate what you need the student to do WITHOUT getting on their horse and doing it yourself. This is where the skill comes in. I know lots of riders, who can feel what a horse is doing or about to do when they are riding it, and know instinctively what to do to fix it, but are not good at being able to see that when they are not riding the horse. Some people find this easy and some people don't.

POTENTIAL INCOME
The average cost and duration of a riding lesson ranges dramatically. From NZ$35 (GBP£17/US$21) for ½ hour up into the thousands for well known or famous instructors.

On average I would say the average riding lesson cost around NZ$60-80 (GBP£29-38/US$37-48) for 45-1hr. Depending on how many lessons you give per week will determine how much you can earn. If you give lessons on your horses then the cost of keeping your horses for this purpose will need to come off that cost.

I charge around NZ$125 (GBP£60/US$75) hour for a private one on one lesson at my facility. Note I do not provide horses for people to do lesson on. This cost is when they bring their horse to me for a lesson. I am able to charge this amount because I have both horsemanship skills/qualifications (Licensed 3 star Parelli Natural Horsemanship Professional) as well as significant teaching skills. I hold a certificate in Adult Teaching (from a National Teachers College) as well as having spent years learning to be a great teacher/instructor completing courses on teaching/instructing and working as a corporate training consultant.

I teach up to 12 lessons a week and always in the afternoons which leaves me free to work with my horses in the mornings. Some weeks I teach only 6 lessons and other weeks I teach 12 making a total of NZ$600-1,200 (GBP£288-576/US$357-714) week from this option alone. When I teach group lessons, the cost decreases per person to NZ$80 (GBP£38/US$48) per person but because there are two or more people in the lesson, the overall income increases to NZ$160 (GBP£77/US$95) per hour or more. Teaching groups of people requires more skill than teaching individuals as you have to have the ability to work with groups or multiple people at one time.

If I travel to lessons, I charge a travel fee otherwise you can end up driving all over the countryside, spending all your income on gas and not actually making any money.

The better your teaching ability and the more equestrian skills you have the more you can make.

Pro's
- This option has the potential to be a good income earner

- There is no outlay required on a daily (other than the initial outlay to gain the skills) to teach
- This is a very flexible option as you can choose your days and hours of work
- You get to work a range of people and horses
- There is a big call for instructors – I am constantly seeing people advertise on social media looking for an instructor to help them with a range of things
- Becoming a great instructor is a great way to build a client base that you can then tap into for other options outlined in this book

Con's

- Not all instructors work for all students – sometimes the style of the instructor simply doesn't suit the student. Its nothing personal, its just what happens
- This is a very active type of income in that it requires to you to do it in order to make any money and you don't get paid when you are sick
- Sometimes it can take a while to build up a client base for this option
- You need to be good at something ideally a discipline AND be good at teaching to really good at this
- If you are going to provide horses for people to take lessons on, there can be significant cost keeping these horses, fit and suitable for people to take lessons on
- If you are going to allow people to use your 'good' horse(s) to take lessons on, be aware that your horses will suffer because of this. They are likely to become duller/not as responsive and less enthusiastic, the more they are ridden by people with lesser skill

WHAT YOU NEED TO GET STARTED AND BE ABLE TO DO THIS

Ideally you will be reasonably good at an equestrian discipline or something to do with horses and/or be a great teacher before you embark on this option. You can do this without owning or having access to a facility if you are prepared to travel to clients which also makes this a great option.

You could take night classes or do an instructor course to help with your teaching skills.

A word of advise here, don't try and be all things to all people. Its easy to think you can teach anyone anything, but because word of mouth advertising is one of the most cost effective and efficient ways to gain clients, you are far better to do one thing well, than try and say you are good at teaching lots of things and then do a poor job. That is a really fast way to loose clients.

A great website helps immensely. There are also lots of social media groups you can advertise your services on as well as advertising in your local supermarket. Many of these ways to advertise are free which really helps.

I found one of the best ways to get clients is to offer lessons for free. I did this when I first started and of the 50 people I gave free lessons to, 49 of them became regular paying clients thereafter.

Animal Aunts/Holiday Accommodation for Horses

WHAT IS IT?
When horse owners go away on holiday or for work, they need someone to take care of their horses. If you don't have a friend or family member that can do this, it can be extremely difficult to find someone with the skills to do this and that's where this service comes in. There are multiple ways to offer this service including offering daily visits to a clients property to check on, feed and care for their horses or having their horse(s) to stay at your property for a short term period or moving in and staying onsite (Horse Sitting) at the clients property to look after their horses at their own property.

POTENTIAL INCOME
If we break this into three categories:
1. Visiting Horse Carer (otherwise known as Animal Aunts) – visiting and caring for horses/pets/any animals at the owners property while they are away: - Examples of what people charge for this is NZ$15 (GBP£7/US$9) per day for the first horse/animal and then NZ$5 (GBP£2.4/US$3) for each extra horse/animal thereafter e.g. 2 horses = NZ$20 (GBP£10/US$12) per day PLUS a milage cost – Standard milage rate = UK GBP 45p, USA$0.585mile, NZ IRD standard milage rate = $0.83km. So someone living 10miles away from you would pay NZ$16.60 (GBP£9/US$11.70 = $0.585 x 20miles/10miles each way) for milage as well as the daily rate. Total cost for 7 days = NZ$256 or GBP£10 x 7 plus £9 x 7 (milage) = £133 for 7 days care of 2 horses (US$221.90).
2. Having the horses stay at your property short term: - Example = First 7 days NZ$25 (GBP£12/US$15) per day, thereafter NZ$20 (GBP£10/US$12) per day (hay and feed not included in either of these).   Note this is pasture care, box care = NZ$40

(GBP£20/US$24) per day. So Total cost for 7 days for two horses excluding hay and feed = NZ$350 (GBP£168/US$208).
3. Horse Sitting (moving into the owners property and caring for the horses and any other animals onsite while they are away): - I don't have rates for this as its normally negotiated between the owner and the horse sitter as it is very dependant on what care you need to provide for the horses.

This gives you an idea, that it can be quite lucrative offering this service especially if you are offering it in conjunction with other services. I have offered this service numerous times to clients and it has worked out extremely well especially when the clients horses come to my property and I just look after them when I am looking after my own.

Pro's

- You can work this around other services you offer
- You get to work with a lot of different horses and people
- Anyone with the skills to take care of a horse can do this
- The need for this service is increasing

Con's

- Not all owners pay their bills in a timely manner, so ensure you have a boarding contract completed in advance if the horses are going to be boarding at your property a contact of agreement of what services you will provide and how you will be paid, prior to starting work as a horse sitter or visiting horse carer
- In the event of one of the horses/animals getting injured while you are taking care of them, you need to ensure you have this is writing as to what they want you to do. Be very clear about this, as some horse owners refuse to pay vet bills if they don't think the vet should have been called
- Ensure you have the correct insurances for this in your country

- Working with horses, even caring for them be dangerous. You need be aware of what is going on around you and consistently work to ensure you stay safe

What you need to get started and be able to do this

If you are going to offer these services, you need to either have a property suitable to board horses while owners are away on holiday and the ability to take care of the horses or you need to have a reliable vehicle you can use to visit the horses you are looking after each day. Advertising on local equestrian social media sites is a good way to get your services out there. You can also create a basic website offering your services, but I have found that generally for this type of service, once you get a couple of clients who love your services, more come by word of mouth.

As previously stated, ensure you have the correct insurances to cover you for this type of service.

Breaking in horses or Starting them under saddle

WHAT IS IT?
Breaking in horses or starting them under saddle is taking a horse that has never been ridden before and educating it understand how to respond when a human sits on its back and asks it to do the basics of walk, trot, canter, stop and turn. Some trainers have a set frame that they work to e.g. they take a horse for four or six weeks and aim to get a set number of things completed with your horse like standing for mounting and dismounting, walk and trot and sometimes canter established, turning softly and stopping. Other trainers take horses for a set amount of time e.g. 3 months and then achieve in that time frame what the horses is capable of doing – it may get to the end of the 3 or 6 months doing a lot more than one who is with a trainer for only 4-6 weeks or it may not depending on the needs of the horse. Both options have pros and cons. How you offer this would need to depend on how you like to break in horses

POTENTIAL INCOME
How much you can earn from this is again dependant on how many horses you can take to break in an any one time or over the course of a year. I know for some trainers this is all they do and for others they do this in conjunction with a number of other options listed in the book. As you will see from the prices quoted by 5 separate trainers, the prices vary greatly. Also I know a number of the trainers do not take horses through the winter or if they do they only take one or two as they cannot guarantee being able to work the horses every day due to adverse weather conditions. This said I know some trainers work on taking 4 horses every other month (some take them every month, but this doesn't leave any time for if a horse needs a few days off due to soreness or unsoundness), effectively taking approximately 20 horses to start a year. 20 x NZ$3,000 (GBP£1,439/US$1783) = NZ$60,000

(GBP£29,000/US$35,661) per year. This is a good income especially if it is done in conjunction with other options listed in this book.

<u>Here are some of the prices I have been quoted for this service:</u>

Trainer 1 - NZ$350 (GBP£168/US$208) week plus feed and hay for a minimum of 4 weeks

Trainer 2 - On average, starting takes 6 weeks, depending on your horse and where you'd like them up to. We have many clients selecting an 8 week start which is an option on the booking form, this allows for a little more space in the program and a more established end result for those horse that the client thinks would benefit from it. Prices vary depending on length of stay, but 6 weeks works out at NZ$3,450 (GBP£1,675 /US$2030).

Trainer 3 - The cost to have a horse started under saddle is NZ$517 (GBP£250/US$304) per week. As noted above, horses are worked five days per week (usually Monday-Friday). Payment Terms, invoiced on a weekly basis for the following week (so payment is always one week in advance). Payment is required on receipt of the invoice to ensure that payment is made prior to work being done each week. Other Costs ♣ Hay is to be supplied by you (approximately four bales per week); if you are unable to supply hay we can supply and add the cost to your invoice each week. You are also most welcome to supply hard-feed if your horse is normally hard-fed.

Trainer 4 - NZ$260 (GBP£125/US$155) per week inc hay.

Trainer 5 - The cost of the training will be paid in full on the day of collection after training has been completed. Breakdown of costs: a) NZ$3,680 (GBP£1,787/US$2,166) 4 week duration. If the TRAINER feels the horse requires further training this will be negotiated with the OWNER, at a rate of NZ$103 (GBP£50 /US$60) per hour. This trainer paddocks the horses in small herds – if you want your horse paddocked individually there is an extra charge of NZ$10 (GBP£5/US$6) per day. Any additional costs (vet fees, farrier etc) will be charged as required.

Trainer 6 - Includes work, feed, hay & paddock. Flat fee (Approx. 8 weeks) to teach your horse the following: To be caught, led, tied up, washed, covered & to present to farrier, vet, dentist and other health professionals. To learn to be patient, trusting and confident. At the end of his education, you will see him relaxed, being confidently handled and working around our track in walk, trot and canter. Breaking-In Filly or gelding in Shared Paddock Flat fee NZ$2,850 (GBP£1,367/US$1693) Breaking-In Colt or individual paddock. Flat fee NZ$3,050 (GBP£1,463/US$1813).

Pro's

- There is good money to made doing this
- You get the opportunity to ride and work with a huge range of horses
- You get to meet a large range of owners who can become clients for other options listed in this book

Con's

- Some horses can be very difficult break in/start under saddle – some trainers will not start horses over the age of 5 as the older a horse is, generally the harder they are to start under saddle
- The risk of injury is higher than most other options listed in this book but that can be negated somewhat by taking a little more time and only starting horses under the age of 5
- Horses can sustain injuries during the breaking in process so you would need to ensure you have proper insurance cover for this or get the owners to sign that they accept you will everything in your power to ensure the horses do not get injured but that you take no responsibility for it if they do
- If the owner of the horse you are breaking in/starting is not as a good as a rider as you, when you give the horse back to its owner, the owner can get bucked off or injured and blame you

– I know some trainers take extensive video footage whilst the horse is in training with them to show how the horse worked for them. This can be useful if you are ever taken to court because of the way the hose acts after it returns to its owner. I also know many trainers that won't return a horse to its owner after starting without a thorough handing over process where the owner watches the horse being ridden and then the owner rides the horse at least once prior to it going home.

What you need to get started and be able to do this
You need to have excellent riding and general horsemanship skills to be able to do this well. I also know the trainers who are very good at this, have a very thorough structured process that each horse goes through, so they know that they have dotted their I's and crossed their t's with each and every horse they break in/start.

You will need to have space to be able to care for and keep the horses while they are being started by you.

Social media is a great place to generate clients for breaking in/starting horses under saddle. Advertise you have availability and to contact you for costs.

You will need a contract for the owners to sign prior to you taking their horses for breaking in/starting to ensure they agree to pay and know what you will and will not do with their horse.

Breed Horses to sell

WHAT IS IT?
This is about breeding horses to sell. Many people do this or big or small scales. Professional studs can breed hundreds of foals each year or you can just breed one or two every year or two.

In order to do this you need to have the space (grazing), time and money to not only set yourself up to breed either with a mare(s) and/stallion(s). You also need to be ok selling horses as this can be hard for some people.

The key to making a success of this option, is to choose a breed of horse that people want to buy. I know a number of people that are breeding a specific breed of horse because they love that breed, but there is little or no market for that breed of horse in the country they are breeding it, which makes selling the resulting foals difficult if not impossible especially if you are hoping to make a profit out of it. Choosing a popular breed is a good way to start but you also need to keep up to date with what the market is doing and ensure you don't keep breeding if the market has dried up.

Here in New Zealand at the moment there is a strong market for good quality Warmbloods as well as Gypsy Cob type horses but little or no market for Standardbreds or Thoroughbreds. New Zealand Thoroughbreds were very sort after a few years ago as eventers, but that market is not quite a strong now. Industries and times change, but if you want to be able to sell your resulting foals, they need to be a popular breed.

POTENTIAL INCOME
Currently in New Zealand a good quality Warmblood weanling sells for between NZ$10,000-$25,000 (GBP£4,800-£12,000/US$5,915-$14,788) depending on its breeding, how successful other horses bred by that stud have been, confirmation and how well it is marketed. Stud fees for stallions differ considerably depending on if you are using frozen

semen from a world-renowned sire or using locally bred stallion. A top dressage stallion could cost upwards of NZ$10,000 (GBP£4,800/US$5,915) for frozen semen and then you have to pay to have your mare inseminated which can range from NZ$600-$6,000 (GBP£288-£2,880/US$355-$3,550) which needs to be added onto the cost of the resulting foal. Lesser expensive stallions service fees could be as low as NZ$1,000 (GBP£480/US$592) which is a lot cheaper but obviously the resulting foal will not necessarily be worth as much, as a foal from a world-renowned sire.

You also need to take into account the cost of taking care of the mare and foal. And there are no guarantees of getting a live, well conformed foal at the end of the day. Ask any breeder and they will likely tell you that even if you do your homework on what is likely to breed well together, that does not mean that you will get a top quality healthy foal. I have personally bred around 50 foals and have found that there can be a problem with three foals in a row which could be during the pregnancy, the foaling or with the foal itself and then you can have another 10 foals in a row without a single problem or confirmational issue. It's a bit of a lottery.

And the other thing to remember is you need to have a good quality mare to breed in the first place. If I have learnt one thing from running a stud for 30 years, it is that if you have a poor-quality mare, be it her confirmation, temperament or pedigree you are more likely to breed a poor quality foal. And make no mistake if your mare or the sire have a bad temperament or behavioural issues, there is a much higher chance the foal will have those same issues. That does not necessarily make for a very saleable foal. If you have to money to invest in good quality mare(s) and stallion(s) you can do very well out of this option.

Pro's

- Once you get your mare in foal and then apart from looking after her, there is very little work to do until the foal is born
- You can choose who and what you breed

- There are always people looking for good quality foals
- Producing a great foal is an amazing experience
- As stated above, there is very good money to made out of this option if you have the funds to purchase great quality mares and stallions/semen

Con's

- It can be a complete lottery at times if you don't start off with a great mare and a good stallion as to what you end up with and as mentioned above, even if you do start with a great mare and stallion sometimes you don't end up with a great foal
- Foal could die – I have bred around 50 foals and have lost two of them. One at 7 days old and the other at a month old. In both cases it was a random birth defect that couldn't be changed but it didn't make us feel any better and the vet fees involved in trying to save the foals were considerable
- Training the foal to lead, tie and load onto a horse float/trailer takes skills, patience and a level horsemanship that you may or may not have
- Foals are notorious for hurting themselves as they don't have a worldly knowledge to know how to keep themselves safe – they run into and fall through fences, they get into things they shouldn't, they are like puppies, you need to make sure you have a safe property and fencing to ensure your investment stays safe

What you need to get started and be able to do this

You will need a good mare and access to a good stallion or semen. You will need facilities to care for the mare while in foal and somewhere safe to raise foal once it is born. You will need a level of capital to invest in the service fee for the stallion and need to be prepared for vet bills for the foal should you need it.

You will need to research what breed types of horses are currently most sort after and you will need to know where they mostly advertised and what they are selling for in your area. This is reasonably easily researched on the internet.

You will need the skills to foal the mare or have the funds to send the mare to someone for the foaling.

You will need the skills to train the foal to lead, tie up, pick up its feet and load onto a horse trailer. These skills can be learnt, but because foals learn extremely fast and we ideally don't want to teach them anything we don't want them to know, it would be good to practice/learn these skills in advance of your foal being born.

Build and sell Obstacles and/or Show Jumps

WHAT IS IT?
This is where you build and sell obstacles that can be used for horses such as pedestals and bridges or build and sell show jumps. I have built and sold pedestals and bridges and know a number of people that have built and sold various different types of show jumps. From wings/side stands to fillers to poles.

With equestrian disciplines such as Cowboy Challenge and Mountain Trail courses becoming more popular, obstacles such as pedestals and bridges are becoming increasingly more popular and there is always a ready market for show jumps.

My husband and I just started building them. He is a bit of a handyman and I grew up with a builder for a father, so had a pretty good idea of how to go about it. Our biggest thing for building the obstacles was to make sure they were safe and would hold the weight of a horse. We probably over engineered ours, but I would rather that, that have one collapse under a horse and rider. Our obstacles had huge horses on them, with no problems at all.

POTENTIAL INCOME
The income potential for this option varies depending on how many obstacles or jumps you make and have available for sale. We were able to make a pedestal for around NZ$100-$200 (GBP£48-£96/US$60-$120) and then sell them for NZ$250-$600 (GBP£120-£288/US$148-$355) each. Bridges cost a little more to make because they required more timber, around NZ$200-$350 (GBP£96-£168/US$118-207) and then we sold them for NZ$500-$1,000 (GBP£240-£480/US$296-$592) each.

Show jumps wings generally sell for NZ$250 (GBP£120/US$148) pair (costing around NZ$100 (GBP£48/US$60) to make) or up to NZ$1,000 (GBP£480/US$600) (costing around NZ$400 (GBP£192/US$237) to make) for extremely high-class sets.

If you make and sell 4 obstacles per month, making NZ$150 (GBP£72/US$89) = NZ$600 (GBP£288/US$355) per month or at the higher end you could make 4 x NZ$400 (GBP£192/US$237) = TOTAL of NZ$1,600 (GBP£769/US$946) per month. This being similar for show jump wings.

Pro's
- You can do this anytime you have spare time
- This is something you can work around any other services you already offer
- Once you get the hang of this, you can build yourself some great obstacles

Con's
- You have to make sure anything you build is safe and will take the weight of a horse – if it was to break or collapse you could be liable for any injuries
- The cost of timber has gone up in recent times, making it more expensive to build the obstacles and jump stands but if you shop around you can still get some good deals
- You have to make sure people pay you for the products prior to them taking delivery, otherwise if they don't pay you, you could be out of pocket

What you need to get started and be able to do this
My husband and I started by finding some obstacles and jump stands we liked and then used them as a pattern to build others. This could be a useful way to start for you too.

Once you decide what you are going to build and how you are going to build them, then you need to decide how much you are going to sell them for and advertise.

Equestrian social media sites on the internet, are a great place to sell this type of product.

Buying and Bringing On/Upskill

WHAT IS IT?
I have found the biggest market for horses is always for the bomb proof or super safe type of horses. They are the hardest to find and they are always VERY expensive. E.g. NZ$10,000-$20,000 (GBP£4,800-£9,600/US$5,915-$11,830) is not uncommon.

Often this type of horse is older, and they have become safe and reliable over the course of many many years. I have also found that if you can find kind good hearted horses who are willing, you often add to their education and then sell them on for a handsome profit.

I know a farm in the USA where this is all they do. They look for good horses generally priced less that NZ$5,000 (GBP£2,400/US$2,957) and then put them through a thorough horsemanship program to produce safe usable horses and then sell them 6-12 months later for a very handsome profit. They have been doing this for years and have a such a fantastic reputation, if anyone wants a really solid good horse, they are one of the first places to look. They are not horse traders, they are there to help horses become great horses and thereby making a great partner for some lucky person.

When I say safe usable horses, I am talking about horses that are easy to take anywhere, do anything with and good in most situations including in different environments. This can take some time to achieve but it most certainly can be achieved when you start with a nice horse and you have good skills and are not in a rush.

POTENTIAL INCOME
How much you can earn from this is dependent on how many horses you have the time to do this with.

To give you a ballpark figure on this, I have found by looking around in New Zealand, good horses can be purchased for between NZ$3,000-$8,000 (GBP£1,440-£3,843/US$1,775-$4,732). Once put through a thorough horsemanship program where they are good to do most anything with and be ridden happily just about anywhere, they can be sold for between NZ$8,000-$25,000 (GBP£3,843-£12,000/US$4,732-$14,788).

P‍RO'S
- There is a huge sense of achievement when you produce a horse like this and sell it to someone who really appreciates it
- If you have good horsemanship skills this can be relatively easy to do even though it can take some time
- There can be good money to be made doing this

C‍ON'S
- Good horses can be difficult to find and you have to know what you are looking for – I have found that just because a horse appears calm and quiet that does not necessarily mean that is the case. You need to have to the skills to know what you are looking at and test the horse thoroughly before you purchase them
- Not all horses turn out great – some horses have some behavioural issues that you were not aware of when you purchased them that make them not as easy to sell
- Sometimes it can take a while to sell a really good horse for really good money
- You have to be ok selling horses – this is not something I enjoy doing but it may be something you are fine with. I know some people who do this, know that even though they don't like this part of the process, it is a small price to pay for them being able to live their lives working with horses each and every day

W‍HAT YOU NEED TO GET STARTED AND BE ABLE TO DO THIS
You need to have very good riding and horsemanship skills to be able to do this well.

You need to learn the best place(s) to buy and sell horses in your area/country.

You need to have enough cash to get started/around NZ$3,000-$6,000 (GBP£1,440-£2,880/US$1,775-$3,549) ideal to be able purchase the first horse you are going to bring on and you need to have the space and resources to be able to afford to care for it while you work with it.

You need to find a good horse to begin this with – note I have found that cold blooded horses e.g. anything with Clydesdale in it (Clydie cross) is a good general place to start looking. Although Clydesdales can be very sensitive they are also generally quite a quiet, friendly, laid back breed of horse and one that seems to be quite popular in the marketplace.

Buying and Selling Horse Feed and/or Hay

WHAT IS IT?

Buying and then selling horse feed and or hay is a great additional income source. Effectively you find the wholesalers of the horse feed you use, buy some in and then sell it at a profit. I know a number of people with horses who have very successfully added this on as an income generating option, to what they already doing.

The closer a horse owner can buy their horse feed to where they live, the easier and more cost effective it is for them which. So if you have to travel a good distance to purchase your horse feed, then it is highly likely other horsey people in your area have to do the same and would be very keen to purchase from you if you offered this service.

You will initially need to source suppliers, but Google has made this a lot easier and most feed has contact details of the manufacturer on the packaging. You will also need somewhere to store the feed, ideally vermin proof and then somewhere to sell it. I know a number of feed shops that keep their extra feed in shipping storage containers that are vermin proof. Great vermin traps are readily available now, which makes the control of vermin less of a problem than it used to be.

I know a number of feed shops, that when they opened they just sold the feed out of their garage or a shed. It doesn't have to be a purpose-built building especially initially.

For this option you will need to outlay some initial capital to purchase your initial stocks.

POTENTIAL INCOME

I do not have income figures for selling bags of feed as this varies enormously but we do make and sell hay every year. We sell small square conventional bales as well as large rounds of hay. We have also sold Lucerne as well as meadow hay.

We sold approximately 250 bales of hay each year or around 25 – 30 large rounds of hay. How much we made each year depended a bit on the year, but we did make money every year, just some years we made more than others.

We paid between NZ$3-$5 (GBP£1.44-£2.40/US$1.77-$2.96) per bale to get the small bales made and then sold them for between NZ$7 (GBP£3.36/US$4.14) and NZ$15 (GBP£7.20/US$8.87) each. On a slow year or a year where there was abundant feed we made approximately NZ$1,000 (GBP£480/US$592) and on a year when there wasn't a lot of feed around we made around NZ$2,500 (GBP£1,200/US$1,479) which was a nice addition to the other income sources we had.

By selling individual bags of feed, you stand to make a lot more than that.

Pro's

- There are always horse owners looking to buy feed both bags of hard feed and hay
- Particularly if you are selling hay, you can work it totally around when it works for you to sell it
- This is an excellent way to keep physically fit and healthy – lifting and shifting hay or bags of feed
- If you are already making hay for yourself, if you can make a bit more than you need, this is a great income earner

Con's

- If you are selling bags of feed, you have to be open at set times – although you can work this around your other commitments
- If is a physical job lugging hay and feed around
- It can take a while to figure out exactly which types of horse feed your locals want to buy but if you stock what you use, that is a great place to start
- You have to stay on top of rodent control or they will eat your profits

WHAT YOU NEED TO GET STARTED AND BE ABLE TO DO THIS

You will need some initial capital to be able to begin this option. Either to buy in bags of feed or pay someone to bale extra bales of hay for you. This is obviously recuperated when you sell the hay or feed, but is required at the outset.

You will need somewhere to store the feed you are going to sell as well as somewhere to sell it from.

You will need to advertise in your local horse community. Great places to advertise are at your local pony club or putting flyer under windscreen wipers at any local horse shows. As well as this, advertising on local social media sites will also help. And ensure you have the correct insurances to run this type of operation in your country.

Buying horses for other people

WHAT IS IT?
I have been contracted to do this numerous times. This is where you are paid to go and find a suitable horse for a person or company. In my case I did both. I brought horses on contract for a Trekking centre and went and found suitable horses for individuals as well.

There are many people who simply don't know what they are looking at, haven't got the experience or they can't read a horse as in its confidence level, if it is happy, stressed, worried, about to explode or simply green or lacking education. The trekking centre that contracted me had previously used a number of 'Horse' people to go and look at horses for them but they kept ending up with unsuitable horses because the individuals were seeing a horse that looked calm to someone lacking real horsemanship knowledge, but in reality the horses they were looking at were only just holding it together and when they got to the trekking centre, they lost it completely and were completely unsuitable. So I travelled all around the countryside being paid for my time and travel to look at and try different horses. The same for individuals looking for a suitable horse, particularly those who were looking for a really 'Safe' horse. Those types of horses are harder to find and you have to know what you are looking so again off I went being paid to find and ride horses. When it comes to a 'Safe' horse, for me I can discern a lot from talking to the owner and even more by watching the horse with the owner even before I ride it. And then when I get in the saddle I pretty much know after a few strides if the horse is going to be suitable. In order to do this option, you need to have that level of skill. Just being able to ride a horse, isn't enough especially when you spending someone else's money.

POTENTIAL INCOME
How this worked for me with the trekking centre was that I was asked at any given time to go and purchase up to X number of horses,

generally 2-4 at a time. I was given a budget to spend per horse which ranged from NZ$6,000-$8,000 (GBP£2,882-£3,842/US$3,549-$4,732) per horse so it was a healthy budget to find good solid gelding horses as they only purchased geldings. I was then paid NZ$100hr (GBP£48/US$59) hour to try a horse out/ride it. I was also paid NZ$50 (GBP£24/US$30) hour to find/source horses and invoiced the company each week. Over the course of a couple of years I purchased quite a few horses for them. Each horse would end up costing them between NZ$500-$1,000 (GBP£240-£480/US$296-$592) extra for my fees, but they knew they were getting good horses. And just about every single horse worked out really well for them.

I have also been contracted by quite a few individuals to do the same thing/find them a suitable horse. As previously mentioned, they were generally looking for 'Safe' horses. My charges were the same as above and in nearly every instance the outcomes were very good.

You have to be 100% honest about your hours as if you are not, you run the risk of having your contract cancelled.

As you can see this option is not a huge income earner, but what I found is, it was a great 'add-on' business that filled in my quiet times and allowed me to still make money when I wasn't busy with other things.

Pro's

- This is a great way to earn money from riding a huge range of horses
- You get to meet interesting people and ride some gorgeous horses
- This is quite flexible/you can fit it in around other things you are doing
- This is a fun way to get to ride a range of horses

Con's

- You have to come up with a system of things to check and test before you get on the horse. I found out that some owners are not particularly honest when it comes to telling you everything about the horse they are trying to sell. I would not ride a horse unless I had seen the owner ride it first and this saved by butt on several occasions when the owner got bucked off their supposedly super quiet horse
- You have to come up with a list of questions to ask particularly around any previous sickness, health issues or injuries the horse has had. This is the only thing I got caught out on, purchasing a horse for the trekking company that had an undisclosed significant issue that rendered the horse ultimately unusable. Wherever possible get a vet check done to try to ensure you cover every single base you can, that the horse you are going to purchase for 'whoever' is in fact what you have been led to believe.

WHAT YOU NEED TO GET STARTED AND BE ABLE TO DO THIS

Firstly advertise that you do this. Again social media is a great way to get your name out there. You could also contact trekking companies or dude ranch operations directly to offer your services.

Think about and work a system including questions to ask that will allow you to be as thorough as possible when it comes to finding out everything you possibly can about the horse you are looking to purchase. Don't just believe what owner says, see if you can cross check everything or test it in some way.

Clinician giving Lessons, Clinics or Camps

WHAT IS IT?
Clinicians have become very popular in the last 20 years. Prior to that there was just one or two. A clinician is effectively someone who is a highly skilled horseman or successful and or knowledgeable equestrian who travels around giving Clinics on the different Horsemanship or Equestrian discipline specific topics.

Clinics can be anything from a few hours to days or weeks. Clinic topics range from very specific topics such as trailer loading right through to riding a cross country course or even how to show a specific breed of horse. The topic range is endless.

A clinician tends to make their money by giving one load of information to many people. Most clinicians travel in order to be able to deliver to enough people to make a good income.

POTENTIAL INCOME
Clinicians can earn anything for NZ$100 (GBP£48/US$59) per day up to NZ$10,000+ (GBP£4,800+/US5,915+) for the really famous equestrian names. I know one not famous but very good clinician in the USA who made over US$200,000 (GBP£165,000/NZ$340,000) in one year working as a clinician. In order to make this much money he travelled every weekend all over the USA as well as delivering week long camps numerous times throughout the year. He was never home but did get to work with a lot of horses and made a very good income doing what he loved. He was also an exceptional horseman and a very good teacher of both horses and humans.

Some clinicians never travel and only deliver one or two clinics a month. On average clinicians charge NZ$200-$400 (GBP£96-£192/US$118-$237) a day for a clinic per person and have anything from 5-50 attend each clinic. So, an average two-day clinic could earn NZ$400 (GBP£192/US$237) x 10 people = NZ$$4,000 (GBP£1,921/US$2,366) per weekend x 52 weeks if you worked every weekend = NZ$208,000 (GBP£100,000/US$123,033) per year. Remembering of course this means you are away from home every weekend and this does not include the cost of your expenses.

Many clinicians use event organisers to advertise and arrange their clinics and pay them a percentage of the income to do this. I have arranged clinics for many clinicians with the average fee being 20% of the total income after expenses. For my 20%, I was responsible for feeding, accommodating and looking after the clinician as well as advertising and getting the students to the clinic. If you do this, you do need to take this off what you might have made out of the clinic if you are a clinician.

PRO'S

- No matter how good you are, your skills will improve because in the process of teaching you will come across horses with problems you have not encountered before
- You will meet some amazing people
- You can earn a significant amount of money doing this
- You will get to spend a lot of time with a lot of different horses
- You will make some incredible lifelong friends doing this

CON'S

- Travelling all the time means you don't get to spend time riding and working with your own horses/your own horses progress can suffer if you don't make this a priority
- Travelling can be extremely exhausting particularly when you are being mentally and physically drained all the time
- You need to ensure you have personal and professional liability insurance to cover you if you are going to do this
- Some horses can be extremely challenging and there is a risk of getting hurt
- Some people can be extremely challenging...

WHAT YOU NEED TO GET STARTED AND BE ABLE TO DO THIS

The key to getting started as a clinician is having skills people want you to teach. But the key to being a successful clinician is to have great teaching skills. You have to make people feel good about their learning if they are going to come back and become lifelong repeat customers. (You can tell I am an adult educator by trade). Many clinicians are great horseman but they can't teach for horse poo. I know two Olympic Gold medallists who are constantly being asked to give clinics and teach people how to do what they do, but neither of them are any good at teaching. One is rude, obnoxious and a bully and the other is an introvert who doesn't like talking to people and likes teaching even less. Both of these very successful people are very good at what they do, as in training and riding horses but they are not teachers and shouldn't teach. But because there is good money to be made doing this, both of them have ended up teaching and neither of them likes doing it one bit.

So firstly work on your horsemanship or discipline specific skills so you have something to teach and secondly learn how to teach. There are lots of educational institutions where you can learn to teaching and presenting skills. If you can learn how to do BOTH of these things you will be a great success as a clinician.

Secondly once you have these skills you need to advertise your services which most people do these via social media and the internet.

Clipping

WHAT IS IT?
Horses get their coats clipped off for a myriad of reasons including aesthetics and practicality. This option is when you provide the service of going around clipping other peoples horses. Clipping is not particularly difficult to do particularly if you only need your horse clipped to make it is easier to groom, but it is more difficult to do a top class show quality job and it is an extremely messy task. For these reasons many people pay someone to clip their horses for them. There are a heap of different types of clips including full body clips, legs only and everything in between. If you are skills clipping horses, this might be something you could consider offering.

POTENTIAL INCOME
It takes approximately 1 ½ hours to complete a full body clip of a horse with the average price for a full body clip being NZ$150 (GBP£72/US$89). If you clipped 2-4 horses per week that is NZ$300-$600 (GBP£144-£288/US$177-$355) per week for 3 – 6 hours work. You also have to factor in the cost of getting your blades of your clippers sharpened. This is not an enormous amount but again if this is done as an 'add on' to other equestrian services you already offer, it is a nice tidy income.

PRO'S
- You can work this around other services you offer
- You get to work with a lot of different horses and people
- Anyone can learn to do this
- You get to become extremely good at clipping because you get a lot of practice
- The need for this service is ever increasing

CON'S

- Some horses are extremely difficult to clip – again good horsemanship skills can really help with this. I helped a couple of girls clip 7 horses. When we went to start, not one of the 7 horses wanted to be clipped. I showed them how teach the horses to stand still and be ok with the clippers. In most cases it took less than 5 minutes for the horses to completely accept the clippers and stand happily without need to be sedated or restrained. See my website for details on how to do this.
- You need to be careful when clipping horses as it is easy to sustain an injury if you are not careful about how you go about this. I have seen horses strike and kick at the clippers and if you happen to get between them and the clippers, you can easily get injured
- You need to make sure your clippers are charged (if you are using rechargeable) and your blades are sharpened ready for use. If your blades are not sharp, they get hot and leave lines when clipping

WHAT YOU NEED TO GET STARTED AND BE ABLE TO DO THIS

To be able to offer this service, you need to have horse clipping skills. As I said above it is not difficult to clip a horse, but it does take some practice. You can learn by taking lessons from someone or watch videos on the internet and then practice.

You need to advertise your services. This can be done on local social media sites.

You need to ensure you have the correct insurances to undertake this type of work.

Competitions like Road to the Horse (USA), Kaimanawa Stallion Challenge (NZ), Thoroughbred OTTB Makeovers (Multiple Countries hold this) or the Extreme Mustang Makeover (USA)

WHAT IS IT?

These types of competitions differ from your standard discipline specific competition with Prize money such as a show jumping, dressage or showing competitions in that they are generally judged on horsemanship and what you can get the horse to do.

These competitions exist all over the world. One of the most famous is 'Road to the Horse' which takes place annually in Kentucky, USA. This competition requires the competitors to start a colt under saddle/break a horse in, over three days but they only have a set amount of time to work with their horse. At the end of the three days there horse has to navigate pretty difficult obstacle course. The competitors are judged each day and then those scores along with how the horse does in the obstacle course decide the winner.

The Extreme Mustang makeover is also held in the USA. With this competition the competitors 100 days to tame and train a wild mustang and then show what it can do at Extreme Mustang Makeover competition finale.

There a number of competitions similar to this all around the world including the Kaimanawa Stallion Challenge in New Zealand. This runs along similar lines.

Many countries also have Thoroughbred Off the Track (OTTB) makeover competitions. These competitions involve competitors taking a Thoroughbred ex-race horse that are no longer any good as a race horse and re training it to be something other than a race horse. Some people teach their horses liberty, some to jump and a host of things in between. Again, the competitors normally have a set amount of time and then showcase what their newly trained ex-race horse, can do. The idea is to save the ex-race horses from slaughter when they are no longer suitable for racing which can happen any time from 2 years of age.

POTENTIAL INCOME
The prize money at these competitions varies significantly. The winner of Road to the Horse which is run in the USA receives US$100,000 (GBP£83,000/NZ$170,000). This particular competition is pretty hard to not only win but also just getting selected to compete is difficult as they only take a select few but do take applications from anyone. This competition also has feeder competitions that you can apply to compete in, which if you win allows you to compete in the major Road to the Horse competition. If you are an accomplished colt starter, these types of competitions can, not only be financially worthwhile but as they are televised they are also a huge advertisement for your skills and services.

The Extreme Mustang Makeover prize money (again run the USA) changes but they were offering US$50,000 (GBP£41,500/NZ$85,000). I am unsure how hard it is to compete in this competition but they have heaps of information online if you are interested.

The New Zealand Kaimanawa (Wild Horse) Freedom to Friendship Stallion Challenge prize money again varies from year to year, with last years prize pool being US$50,000 (GBP£41,500/NZ$85,000) in money and prizes.

Worldwide the OTTB makeover competitions have become popular with the prize money varying from NZ$1,000 - US$100,000 depending on the country it is being run in. These competitions are often included as part of major Equine Entertainment/Education events such as EQUITANA and the like.

PRO'S
- These competitions are a great way to showcase your skills and advertise your services – if people like what you do and the way you do it, there is no better advertisement

- You get to test your skills
- The competitions where you take the horse for re educating for a set period of time, normally allow quite a bit of flexibility where you can fit it in around other things you are doing
- There is often very good prize money for these competitions and not very many competitors, as there are not many trainers with enough skills to compete

Con's

- Sometimes the horse you get can take a lot more time than you were expecting and you have to be prepared to put in the time that the horse needs in order to achieve a great outcome
- The wild horse taming and training competitions require a high level of skill and even then the risk of getting injured working with a wild horse is considerably higher than working with a domesticated horse
- For the competition where there is a grand finale competition there is a risk of putting in a lot of time and effort to the horse you have been allocated and then it getting injured or going lame prior to the final competition – this happened to a number of competitors at last years Kaimanawa Freedom to Friendship Stallion Challenge. The trainer is then out of pocket for the time they invest in the horse. Even though the trainer doesn't end up with any prize money they do still get a good bit of publicity during the course of the event. Also even if you don't end up winning any prize money for whatever reason, you have helped a horse. That may seem trivial but for those of us who love horses, that is a great consolation prize.

What you need to get started and be able to do this

Firstly you need to investigate what competitions are available in your region/country and which ones you have the skills to compete in. Next you need to find out what the competitor criterial is and if you meet it.

You will then need to apply to compete and if accepted, you are on your way!

Also before you embark on these types of competitions, consider what products or services you want to advertise as that is one of the big bonuses that come out of these types of competitions, is the free advertising for you receive before, during and after the competition. Sometimes the advertising alone is worth the investment of time, even if you don't win any prize money.

Equine body worker/Chiropractor

WHAT IS IT?
In more recent times it has become more widely known that competition horses or horses in general are athletes and function considerably better if they are treated as such than 'just a horse'. What I mean by this is if you are training for a marathon, generally you will consider things like a nutrition, fitness and training. You will look to have your body in the best physical condition to be able to run the marathon. You may consult a massage therapist or chiropractor if things don't feel right or even if you just think they might help. Some people will consult a physiotherapist or personal trainer. These are now the types of professionals Horse owners consult for their horses. I personally have used a wide range of professionals who offer different equine therapy options including an equine chiropractor, an equine massage therapist and an equine therapist who does a combination of chiropractic and massage therapy for my horses.

Learning to be able offer one of these services is what this option is about. Some people who offer this service are self-taught and others undergo considerably training to gain qualifications to be able to do what they do. If you Google 'Equine Bodywork' you will get a huge range of options that you can investigate. This is definitely a growing industry.

POTENTIAL INCOME
The costs of these services vary considerably depending on what is being offered and by whom.

Charges for an Equine Chiropractor in New Zealand is around NZ$95 (GBP£46/US$56) per session plus milage. This chiropractor can see 10+ horses a day = NZ$950 day (GBP£460/US$560).

Costs for Equine Therapy in New Zealand average around NZ$100 (GBP£50/US$60) per session plus milage, so similar to the above. And one Equine Osteopath here in New Zealand charges NZ$150 (GBP£75/US$90) per session.

There are a huge range of services that fit into this category. The above figures give you an indication of what is possible.

Pro's
- You can work this around other services you offer
- The need for this service is increasing
- You get to work with a huge range of horses and people
- You get to help a lot of horses

Con's
- Some horses can be difficult to work with but good horsemanship skills can help with this
- You generally need to undertake some training in order to offer this service which involves time by way of taking, studying and qualifying in a particular specialist area and there will be a cost
- You need to have to the correct insurances in case you cause some unexpected injury to a horse you are working on or sustain an injury yourself when working with a horse

What you need to get started and be able to do this

Firstly you need the skills to be able to offer this service.

Next is ensuring you have the correct insurances to cover you for all eventualities when working someone's horse and finally you will need to advertise your services. Again social media site with an equine focus are a great place to start.

Equine Show Turnout Services

WHAT IS IT?
If you provide Equine Show Turnout services you provide services including plaiting of manes and tails, pulling tails, doing makeup for horses, washing and generally preparing horses and ponies for shows or events. Many equestrian disciplines other than showing events require horses to be plaited including Dressage and Eventing. Some individuals who offer this service also offer show day grooming services as well as lessons and clinics.

Many horse owners don't want to plait their horse for an event or simply aren't very good at the skill so want a professional to do it for them.

Although the skills required to provide this service are significant, they are also extremely learnable.   Between online tutorials and taking lessons from someone who is good at this, with practice you can gain these skills reasonably quickly if this option interests you.

POTENTIAL INCOME
On average to have a horses mane and tail plaited, costs around NZ$60 (GBP£29/US$35). It takes around 35 minute to plait a mane and up to an hour to plait a horse mane and tail. Plaiting can be done the night before the show which allows anyone who does this to get around to quite a few properties on a Friday or Saturday evening as most shows or equine events take place on Saturday or Sunday.

If you plait 4 horses a week (and for some shows this can be considerably more) this equals 4 x NZ$60 = NZ$240 week (GBP£115/US$142). This is a service especially when you can add on services such as:-
- Pulling manes/pre show tidy ups – average cost NZ$30-$50 (GBP£14-£24/US$18-$30)
- Tail shaping/cutting – average cost NZ$20 (GBP£10/US$12)
- Washing horses

- Full turn out services – average cost NZ$70-$100 (GBP£34-£48/US$41-$60)
- Plaiting lessons – average cost NZ$60 hour (GBP£29/US$35)

PRO'S
- You can work this around other services you offer
- You get to work with a lot of different horses and people
- You get to become extremely good at what you do because you get to do a lot of it
- The need for this service is ever increasing

CON'S
- Some horses are extremely tricky to deal with and don't like standing still to be washed, have make up put on or have their mane or tail plaited – good horsemanship skills can help with this
- If you are suppling the products, you need to ensure cost of these is factored into your charges as its easy to end up undercharging and not actually make any money
- Some clients will book you in and then cancel at the last minute – this can be alleviated by having them pay in advance and making it non refundable and making bookings on a first come first served basis can also help with this

WHAT YOU NEED TO GET STARTED AND BE ABLE TO DO THIS

To be able to offer this service, you need the skills to wash, plait and prepare a horse for a show. You can take classes on how to do this and you can also watch videos on the internet and learn that way.

Next you need a booking system. This can be done manually to begin with and later on you can move it to an electronic booking system if you want to.

And finally you need to advertise your product. Again a website is well worth building for this type of service as you can show photos of what you can do and offer.

Advertising can be done on local social media sites. You can also contact the local equine breed societies and advertise directly in their newsletter to members. This works extremely well as breeders are always looking for these types of services.

You need to ensure you have the correct type of insurances to complete this type of work.

Facility Hire – Arena, Jumps, Obstacles, a Gallop track or Cross Country Jumps

WHAT IS IT?
This is a great option to take advantage of if you already own or have facilities that people want to use/hire e.g. an Arena and/or Jumps, Round Pens, Obstacles or Cross Country Jumps. People are always looking for places to ride and facilities that they don't personally have free access to. This applies all over the world. I know people who rent out everything from the farm they own to for riders to trail ride over, dressage arenas, indoor and outdoor, Show Jumps, general obstacles, gallop tracks and cross country courses. There is no limit to this. People with horses are keen to hire all sorts of things. I personally have hired out my all-weather outdoor arena, my 800m gallop track and my horse Obstacle course.

POTENTIAL INCOME
Facilities are charged out by the hour, by the day, by the week and by the month. I know one trainer who rents an entire ranch for months at a time to run camps at. I know numerous facilities who rent out their arenas both indoor and outdoor by the hour, day and week. There are lots of options here.

An outdoor arena is normally charged out for one rider NZ$100 (GBP£50/US$60) week and we didn't have to do anything.

These are not huge sums of money but they do add up over time, particularly if you rent out your arenas or facilities when you aren't using them and they are sitting idle anyway.

I know one indoor arena that the owners use Monday – Friday and rent out at weekends. Weekends tend to be when people want to hire them. They charge it out at NZ$250 (GBP£120/US$148) per day, so NZ$500 (GBP£240/US$298) for the weekend and it is hired pretty much every weekend during Spring, Summer and Autumn = 36 weeks @ NZ$500 = NZ$18,000pa (GBP£8,646/US$10,648).

That's an indicator of what's possible.

Pro's

- This is a great way to earn money off the facilities that you have anyway
- You get to meet interesting people
- This option requires minimal time commitment from you so you are free to do other things
- This is also a great way to advertise any other services you offer – as you can put up signs for everyone to see who comes to your property
- There is almost always a market for this

Con's

- Some people who want to hire your facilities can be difficult. They can be slow to come back to your with confirmation of bookings, they change their mind at the last minute and then they run over their time –You need to be very specific particularly around payment. For indoor arenas, I suggest a non refundable deposit followed by full payment being required X days before the hire and if the hire was cancelled within that X day window, they forfeited their payment. Whatever you decide get them to complete a hire document whenever they want to hire the venue.
- Often people don't clean up after themselves (you need to be very specific about this) which means you often have to clean up after people
- You may not like the way people are treating the horses that are using your facilities
- There will be other people on your property

What you need to get started and be able to do this

Firstly you need to have the correct insurances to cover hiring whatever facilities you plan to hire incase of damage to your property or the individuals who are using it.

Secondly you need to have some sort of clear booking system. I had people text me their bookings, followed by making electronic payment. I recorded the bookings in the electronic diary which I checked every morning so I know who was going to be where.

Secondly from a health and safety perspective it pays to have the facility users sight some sort of health and safety briefing document covering any hazards and any responsibilities they have when using your premises. One Equestrian centre where I hired the facilities, had a small shed with sign in and out documents as well as their health and safety requirements that you were required to adhere to, whilst you were on their premises. They also had a payment tin where you placed any cash payments. This system worked extremely well as you were not allowed onto the premises without completing the sign in documents.

Advertising any facilities you have available can be done on notice boards at local shops, as well as social media as well as putting a sign up outside your premises.

Fix and Flick ponies

WHAT IS IT?
Fixing and Flipping ponies is a GREAT way to earn money working with horses. Fixing and Flicking ponies is effectively buying ponies with behavioural and sometimes physical problems, fixing them and then selling the ponies on again. I did this for a number of years. Why ponies? There is always a market for ponies. Children are always wanting ponies and because children grow, their parents are always looking for their next pony. I have also found that ponies are way easier to sell than trying to do this with horses. Also parents are willing to spend large sums of money on their children when many of them won't spend that money on themselves. Some of the issues I found with the ponies I fixed and flicked were:

- Trailer loading issues, which I found easy to sort out – many ponies had simply said no to the child and the parent who wasn't very horsey but when approached by someone with horsemanship skills, they were easy to convince that loading was good idea.
- Bucking – in many cases this was caused by ill-fitting tack/discomfort – I had body work done on the ponies and then did lots of in hand work with them to ensure they were comfortable and many of the bucking problems simply ceased. Others required more work, but with good horsemanship skills, this wasn't difficult to sort out
- Catching – this tended to be one the biggest reasons people ended up selling ponies, they couldn't catch them. That's no fun for the child or the adult when the pony was difficult to catch. I played the Parelli catching game with the ponies and in no time at all they would be following me around. That actually ended up being a great selling point for the ponies. I would always show any potential purchaser how to do that with the pony so the problem wouldn't present itself again.

Potential Income
- How much you can earn from this is dependant on how many ponies you can turn over. I made approximately NZ$1000 (GBP£500/US$600) per pony when I did this. I say approximately because some I made a lot more and others I made less. When I did this I was doing other things as well, but found on average if I put in an hour a day for two weeks, most problems were pretty much sorted. Note some did take longer but others took no time at all. This is dependant on your skill level but if you could turn over a pony every fortnight, you could potentially make NZ$26,000 (GBP£12,488/US$15,379) per year.

Pro's
- There is always a ready market for good ponies
- There were lots of ponies around with problems so easy to find ponies to fix
- I normally made at least a $1000 per pony which is good money especially if you can sort the problem out quite quickly

Con's
- You have to be careful which ponies to purchase – a bad attitude can be difficult to fix unless it is because of a fixable physical issue. I tended to steer clear of anything that had a bad attitude and just purchased the ones that had a behavioural issue that I knew how to fix.
- You need to be small enough to be able to ride the ponies that need time put in, in the saddle
- You need to be able to afford to care for the ponies whilst you are working with them

What You Need To Get Started And Be Able To Do This

You need to have good general horsemanship skills and the ability to diagnose and fix a range of problems that ponies develop such as bucking, trailer loading issues, pulling back etc.

You will also need funds to purchase your first pony or two. I paid anything from $100 - $2,000 for ponies.

Once you have sold each pony and made money, this will become self-funding as it did for me.

Work out how much time you have available, how long you think it will take to fix any ponies given problem and the cost of caring for the pony during that time. This cost needs to be factored in before deciding which ponies to purchase.

I advertised in my local paper for ponies with problems/issues or needing rehoming. This worked brilliantly and I found heaps of ponies by doing this. You could also advertise on social media.

A place to keep them while you work with them

Before you start this, make sure you know where and how ponies are sold in your region – if they are mostly sold in your area on an internet sales platform – make sure you take into account the cost of listing your fixed pony on that platform before deciding on which ponies to buy. You have to be able to make money a pony.

Foaling Attendant

WHAT IS IT?
Stud farms, Veterinary Hospitals and Equine breeding centres need people to watch their broodmares (Foaling attendants) when they are getting close to foaling so they can assist with the birth of the foal if required. They can then also provide immediate medical attention to the foal and mare, again if required.

With the value of foals increasing as access to high quality frozen semen from around the world becomes more readily available, mare owners are working harder to ensure the safe arrival of their foals. Because of this many breeders are choosing to send the mare to a specialist breeding farm where there is 24 hour care and watch on the broodmares. By doing this they can reduce the risk of potential problems during foaling. Many maiden mares (first time mothers) have problems at foaling. As well as this, a reasonably high numbers of foals born from domestic horses, arrive with physical issues, that if addressed early can be easily rectified which is where foaling attendants come in.

Foaling attendants do not necessarily need to be experienced working with broodmares and foals as many of these establishments that provide these services also provide training and/or have you work in a team so that someone with more experience is there to show you what to do, in the event of a problem. Again the key to being able to get one of these roles is to have good horse handling/horsemanship skills which as I have mentioned with other options, is learnable through courses, training or working for a trainer with great horsemanship skills. Another option to obtaining one of these roles is work as a working student for a trainer, where you can learn and gain experience, which then sets you up to apply for one of these roles. I have had stable hands come and work for me and then go on to be foaling attendants after obtaining horsemanship skills.

POTENTIAL INCOME
The gross annual salary of a foaling attendant in New Zealand is around NZ$39,000 (GBP£18,732/US$23,068). Salaries appear to be similar in other parts of the world.

PRO'S
- You get to work with a huge range of horses and people
- You get to help a lot of horses
- You will learn a lot about caring for horses and what can be done to help mares foaling as well as foals
- If you love horses, watching a foal being born is an incredible thing and something you will not forget

CON'S
- Foaling attendants can be a seasonal role only available during spring and summer
- Broodmares can be very protective of their foals so you need to be aware at all times when working with mares and foals
- Some horses can be very difficult to work when they have a baby - good horsemanship skills can really help you with this
- Getting the initial skills required to get the job may take some time and require working for someone experienced with training or handling horses prior be able to get one of these roles

WHAT YOU NEED TO GET STARTED AND BE ABLE TO DO THIS
You will need good horsemanship skills. Ideally if you can get some work on a stud farm, working with mares and foals that would help considerably.

Use Google to search for 'Foaling attendant' roles and also contact Equine Hospitals and ask if they have these roles available and advise you are very keen to secure such a role.

Put together a CV in readiness. There are lots of free CV writing tools on the internet to assist you with this.

Foundation Training

WHAT IS IT?
Lots of trainers have different names for this, but effective after a horse has been broken in/started under saddle comes developing the foundation that will support them throughout their life. The Foundation can develop more advanced ridden skills including starting to work on balance, using their body more biomechanically correctly and contact or starting to work in a frame. It can cover riding in new environments, with other horses or gaining confidence riding out by itself. Foundation training can also cover a lot more on helping the horse to become a good citizen including tying up if this is still not solidified, being washed, further hoof preparation if a horse is still struggling with this or a host of other things. Foundation training is offered either on a per week basis or a 1-3 month contract.

POTENTIAL INCOME
How much you can earn from this is dependant on a couple of things. I have found there are not as many people who are prepared to pay for this service as there are for general schooling or breaking in. Most people will pay to have their horse started/broken in as there is a higher injury risk to themselves, but not pay for its ongoing education as they think they can do this themselves, which many can. But there is still without doubt a market for this. It differs from general schooling as it normally follows on from a horse being started under saddle and generally not discipline specific which often schooling tends to be. I know one trainer who does a lot of foundation training with horses.

Charges are generally similar to those charged for schooling. This is a good income especially if it is done in conjunction with other options listed in this book.

- Trainer 1 - NZ$250 (GBP£120/US$148) week which excludes feed and hay
- Trainer 2 - NZ$195 (GBP£94/US$115) week includes feed but excludes shoeing and teeth
- Trainer 3 - NZ$1,000 (GBP£480/US$592) per month plus feed and hay

Pro's

- Because the people who are prepared to pay for this service generally want a great horse at the end of the day, the horses you get offered for this service are generally really good horses to start with. They are already started under saddle which means there is generally a much lower risk of injury to yourself with this type of training
- You get the opportunity to ride and work with a range of horses
- With this type of service you often have horses for longer so are able to achieve more with them, which can be a lot more fulfilling

Con's

- Owners wanting you to work miracles and achieve the impossible in too short a timeframe – again I know some trainers who agree to take horses for this with a caveat of a one week trial (at the owners expense) so they can determine if what the owner is after is achievable with this horse

What you need to get started and be able to do this

You need to have good riding and general horsemanship skills to be able to do this well. You need to ensure you clearly understand and have a written contract with the owner of the horse as to what they expect you to do, within the timeframe you have the horse. I don't

have any specific examples of this, but again you could use one of the breaking in contracts.
You will need to have space to be able to care for and keep the horses while you work with them.

Social media is a great place to generate clients for Foundation Training. Advertise you have availability and to contact you for costs.

Grazing/Boarding/Agistment/Livery Horse Services

WHAT IS IT?
What this is called differs throughout the world, but effectively it is providing somewhere for other people's horses to live/graze or board. Sometimes it is offering pasture boarding/grazing and sometimes it is offering stable/stall board and sometimes it is offering a combination of the two. Full service options often called Livery or Full Board are one option available, where the owner of the facility/property provides complete care for a horse and the owner just turns up to ride or visit their horse. Other options include a DIY (Do it Yourself), Grazing or Agistment, where the owner of the horse totally cares for the horse and just pays the property/facility owner (you) for the use of the grazing or stall or both. What you offer, depends on what facilities you have available, how much time you have available and how 'hands on or off' you want to be.

POTENTIAL INCOME
How much you can charge and ultimately earn for this service depends on a few factors:-
- How close to a city you live (as this creates more demand) and what other boarding facilities are available in your area.
- What facilities you have available for the boarders to use - The more facilities you have available for the boarders/grazers to use onsite, significantly effects how much you are able to charge. For example if you have an all weather sand arena or an indoor sand arena available for the boarders to use, this not only makes your facility much more inviting but also increases what you can charge. The same goes for access to show jumps, wash down facilities or riding areas.
- What options - Full service or DIY where the owners look after their own horses. you can offer

Examples of charges: Note I have worked the possible incomes on 10 horses. Many of these barns/facilities accommodate considerably more than 10 horses, but this at least gives you an idea of what is possible

1. <u>Example one</u> – Cost is NZ$50 per week (GBP£25/US$30) - This facility check all horses daily, harrow paddocks, clean the water troughs and do all the paddock maintenance regularly. Your horse or pony is fed grass fed and fed baleage/hay in winter, grazed in a suitable mob with our horses, cover removed & replaced as needed etc. Shoeing, clipping & worming can be arranged at competitive prices.
Total per Year for 10 horses is NZ$50week x 10 x NZ$5,000 (GBP£2444/US$3000)

2. <u>Example two</u> – offers safe paddocks with electric top wires. Horses are kept in small groups together. They offer Large outdoor arena 70 x 65m, fully lit, show jumping course, dressage arena with superior soft rubber/sand surface. Indoor arena fully lit (to use outside their riding school hours). Exercise training tracks (600m & 1000m). Grooming tie stalls. Warm water shower for horses. Tack room – locked to store your gear. Feed room. Toilets. Coffee/tea/TV. Float/truck parking. Solarium. They have two options available - OPTION 1 – PART LIVERY - Horses checked daily, hard fed, hayed out and covers changed if required . NZ$18 per day (GBP£9/US$11). Stable can be added at NZ$2 per day (GBP£1/US$1.2). OPTION 2 – FULL LIVERY - All of Option 1, but stable and bedding is provided, horses can be bought in and out and stable will be cleaned . Horses are bought in for shoeing and veterinary attention. NZ$25 per day (GBP£12/US$15). (Both options owners to provide own hard feed and hay)
Total per Year for 10 horses = 10 x NZ$25 x 365 = up to NZ$91,250 (GBP£44,611/US$54,604)

3. <u>Example three</u> – OPTION ONE - FULL LIVERY BOARDING. WHAT'S INCLUDED: Stable and paddock/yard stay. Customised feeding program. Personalised care and grooming. In-hand or ridden exercise upon request. Daily monitoring. Full facility use. Horse truck/float available on request. Weekly rate: NZ$250 (GBP£120/US$148). Total per Year for 10 horses = 10 x NZ$250 x 52 = NZ$130,000 (GBP£64,000/US$78,000)
OPTION TWO – GRAZING - WHAT'S INCLUDED: Safe and secure paddock stay. Personalised care and grooming. Customised feeding program. Daily continual monitoring. Full facility use. Horse truck/float available on request. Yards available for horses with laminitis. Weekly rate: NZ $140 (GBP£68/US$84). Total per Year for 10 horses = 10 x NZ$140 x 52 = NZ$72,800 (GBP£36,000/US$44,000)
4. <u>Example Four</u> – from the USA – this facility had 5 different options – they had 3 different barns which offered different levels of space and comfort for the boarding horses. The horses in the barns also got turned out 6 times a week and the cost varied accordingly from US$700-US$1,000 month. They also offered two pasture boarding options which ranged from US$624-US$570 month. The stall boarders had access to the facilities large indoor arena as well as the outdoor arenas, whereas the pasture boarders only had access to the outdoor arenas.
Total per year for 10 horses = 10 x US$1,000 x 12 = Up to US$120,000 (GBP£98,000/NZ$200,000)
5. <u>Example Five</u> – from the USA – All stalls are a very large 12'x18' and fully matted. Ample shavings cover half of the stall so the hay does not get mixed in with the shavings. Some of the stalls have attached 12x24 runs which are partially matted as well. Rates vary from US$450 per month for pasture only, US$600/$650 for stalls and US$750 per month for stalls with large private paddocks. Other configurations are also available.

Board includes feed, shavings, cleaning, all day pasture turn out, body checks, applying & removing fly masks & blankets, and feeding owner provided supplements. All horses go out on green, irrigated pastures all day in compatible groups. They are fed mainly Orchard grass but customize the diet according to the horse's individual needs with other forage when necessary. All hay is tested, fed up to 5 times/day depending on the horse's condition, work load, time of year and turnout.
Total per year for 10 horses = 10 x US$750 x 12 = US$90,000 (GBP£73,000/NS$150,000)

6. <u>Example Six</u> – This ranch features 310 acres of rolling hills and creek bottom for riding, includes a 150 x 300' outdoor arena, two 60' round pens, two wash racks, and various stalls, corrals and pastures. The facility has a maximum of 30 horses. Specialized care is given to each individual horse's needs whether it is housed in the full care barns, corrals, or out on pasture. Prices range from US$400 per month for stall and pasture boarding to US$215 month for pasture only boarding.
Total per year for 10 horses = 10 x US$400 x 12 = US$48,000 (Note this barn boards 30 horses so potentially up to US$144,000 per year. (GBP£117,000/NS$240,000)

PRO'S

- There are significant sums of money to made with this option
- If you already have the space and facilities, this can be a easy money making option, where you get to work with many horses
- I have had many long term boarders/grazers that were brilliant to deal with, paid on time every week and looked after their horses really well
- This is a great way work with lots of horses
- This is a great way to meet lots of people

Con's

- Sometimes owners don't pay their bill, so you need to have strategies in place to ensure you get paid. These could include legal boarding contracts and/or written agreement with the owners prior to accepting their horses.
- I had a problem with one boarder where she had a contract with me for grazing at our property only and she looked after her own horses. I noticed one day that she hadn't been to feed, water and pick up the manure for her horses. I tried to contact her but she didn't answer her phone or respond to me messages, so I fed and watered her horses (with my feed) and picked up her paddock. This continued for 3 weeks. She effectively just disowned her horses. Without me looking after them, they would have had no food or water and been knee deep in manure. Finally she turned up after three weeks and it turned out she had been sick and didn't bother to get in contact. She wasn't prepared to pay for the food I had feed her horses or the care/time I had had to invest in looking after them. I learnt from that experience you need to have things like that covered in the contact/agreement they sign PRIOR to them arriving with their horses.
- Some owners don't look after their horses they way you would expect them to. This can be negated by ensuring you have a minimum standard of care in the boarding contract/agreement to ensure you don't have to deal with this.
- Some owners treat their horses poorly – again to ensure you are not faced with a cruel or malicious horse owner on your property, ensure you have guidelines in the boarding contact/agreement of what is acceptable and what is not.
- This means you have other people coming onto your property 7 days a week – this is not for everyone
- If you are offering full service care, some horses can be difficult to catch and deal with especially if they get injured and require

attention from a vet – good horsemanship skills can help immensely with this

WHAT YOU NEED TO GET STARTED AND BE ABLE TO DO THIS

You will need a boarding contact/agreement. I decided not to include a sample boarding contact in this book because every country around the world has different legal requirements. If you do a Google search on horse boarding or grazing for horses in your country, you will be able to find numerous examples of boarding contracts that you can use as a starting point. Another option is to seek the advice of a lawyer on this. They can make sure you are covered legally as well as ensuring you are in a position to be able to collect any unpaid fees.

I find advertising on local supermarket noticeboards and on local social media sites are great ways to get your name out there. Word of mouth normally takes over after that. You can also contact any local pony clubs or 4H clubs and let them know you have space available.

Ensure you have the necessary insurances as well as being very clear about what you will and will not do for the horses in your care.

Hoof Trimming

WHAT IS IT?
Horses have to have their feet trimmed every 4-8 weeks. In the wild horse cover an average of 45kms per day which allows their feet to wear away naturally but unfortunately domesticated horses on average only do between 3-15km per day which effectively means their simple don't do enough miles to wear down their feet naturally so they have to have them physically trimmed. A farrier generally does this. A farrier has generally received a level of training on how to both trim and correctly shoe a horses hoof, although not always, some are self-taught. As nearly every single horse requires its hooves to be trimmed, there is an enormous call for this service.

By way of an example of the demand for this service, my husband trained and qualified as a barefoot trimmer. Note this differs from the training a qualified farrier undertakes, in that it covers more in-depth training on how a natural hoof should function and the effects a correctly functioning and incorrectly functioning hoof have on the overall health of the horse. A farrier generally receives more training on how to correctly shoe a horse. The Barefoot trimming qualification my husband undertook included two years of part time study, which included numerous weeklong practical training camps and then was required to pass both theory and physical examinations. Anyone can do this course. Following on from doing this course, he advertised he was available to do hoof trimming and was inundated with requests. I got offered a job in Germany recently and when I mentioned my husband (Tony) was a qualified barefoot trimmer, they advised there was a huge shortage of trimmers in Germany and he would be very welcome. I was recently in Colorado in the USA and someone was trying to find a hoof trimmer or farrier and couldn't get one anywhere. There seems to be a worldwide shortage of people with these skills.

POTENTIAL INCOME

A good trimmer can trim a horses' hooves in anything from 20-40minutes depending on how complex the hooves. The average trim costs NZ$50-$100 (GBP£25-£50/US$30-$60) per trim. When talking to friends in Germany, they advised the average trim there, costs €80 (GBP£70/US$85/NZ143). When trimming my husband could trim up to 10 horses per day which is potentially NZ$500-$1000 (GBP£250/US$300) per day. A good trimmer can trim anything from 25-50 horses per week. Total Yearly Income 25-50 x NZ$50-$100 = NZ$1,250-$5,000 per week x 48 weeks per year = NZ$60,000 - NZ$240,000 (GBP£30,000-117,000/US$36,000-144,000). As you can see good trimmers can make a very good living doing this.

You do need to factor in the cost of replacing your tools e.g. Rasps and Knives.

PRO'S

- You can work this around other services you offer
- You get to work with a lot of different horses and people
- Anyone can learn to do this
- You get to become extremely good at trimming hooves because you get a lot of practice
- You get to stay extremely fit and trim as this is fairly physically demanding
- The need for this service is considerably and ever increasing

CON'S

- Some horses are extremely difficult to trim – some are frightened, some are in pain and struggle to lift their hooves, some have had poor training and effectively taught the wrong behaviours – again good horsemanship skills can really help with this. My husband would work with the horses and there just about wasn't a horse he couldn't trim – I have an online course on how to work with horses that are difficult to trim

their feet and teach them to allow you to pick up and trim their hooves easily – see my website for this
- Working around a horse's hooves can be extremely dangerous. You need be aware of what is going on around you and consistently work to ensure you stay in safe position

WHAT YOU NEED TO GET STARTED AND BE ABLE TO DO THIS

To be able to offer this service, you need to have hoof trimming skills. As I said above anyone can learn to do this. There are courses around that teach it and I know a number of people who have learnt to do this by reading books, watching videos and then practicing a lot. So anyone can learn.

You will need the tools including chaps, clippers, knives and rasps but most cities have a farrier supply shop or these can be purchased online.

Advertising on local social media sites and contacting your local pony club is also a great way to get your name out there. My husband found that word of mouth in the equestrian industry works extremely well once you get going.

Ensure you have the correct insurances to do this work in your country.

Horse Adventure Park

WHAT IS IT?
I have found that as rural roads have become busier with more traffic, many horse people no longer want to ride on the road. They are looking for places they can go and ride, where they and their horses are safe. They are also looking for things they can do that are not necessarily competitive but just fun to have a go at. Effectively a place that allows them to enjoy their horses, in a safe environment where they can do as much or as little as they like.

With this in mind, my husband and I created the 'Horse Adventure Park'. We utilised what our 20 acre property had to offer including a 800 metre training track, previously used for Harness racing training as well as building a range of natural obstacles. We also created a 'Mystery Obstacle' area. The natural obstacles were permanent obstacles such as banks with drops, tunnels, bridges, steps that went up and over a large mound of dirt, a log corner that had some rather large logs positioned in an 'L' shape that the horses had to walk between, ditches, permanent water obstacles as well as a rock pathway with large rocks scattered randomly which needed the horses to pick their way through.

The Mystery Obstacle was made up of generally movable/changeable obstacles, that I changed regularly so the Park was every changing and fresh for regular uses. This included things like rocker bridges, pedestals set up sometimes with flags or just by themselves in different areas of the park, sometimes with flapping obstacles or obstacles the horses had to walk under, over or between such as tarpaulins or soft toys. I came up with also sorts of random obstacles including a kids bubble machine. That actually proved to be one of the most challenging obstacles the horses came across in the Park, because it made a funny sound and produced bubbles extremely randomly. The people who visited the park just loved that obstacle.

We also had a big sand arena and two large round pens that people could use as and how they wanted to.

There are various ways this type of facility can be run. We set it up so that the facility was only open twice a month on a Sunday and then only for a maximum of 2 hours at a time. We allowed a maximum of 25 people to attend during any given 2 hour session and they had to book in and pay in advance. We used 'Eventbrite' which is an online event booking system to manage our bookings which worked fantastically. It was easy to use and required minimal setup and the Eventbrite cost per participant, was minimal.

We had a lot of requests to open the Horse Adventure Park up at other times for people to use, but as I used the facility for teaching as well, we choose to limit it to specific times twice a month. The limited availability meant we were basically fully booked every time we made sessions available. I have no doubt this type of facility could open considerably more than we did, and still be very popular.

POTENTIAL INCOME

We charged NZ$25 (GBP£12/US$15) per horse for each two hour session. We would often run 2 sessions per day 10am – 12noon and 1pm – 3pm. Thus we had a maximum of 50 people per day at NZ$25 each. We made NZ$1,250 (GBP£611/US$748) per day each time we ran it. We ran it approximately twice a month from August to April and were fully booked nearly every time. This equated to around NZ$22,500 (GBP£11,000/US$13,500) per year. We also had riding groups book it out on a regular basis. Which we charged out at the same price.

Right from the start we were inundated with people wanting to come along. Because the attendees were free to come and go as they pleased and didn't have to stay for the whole two hours, people would bring young horses along for ½ an hour and then take them home again. It was a great first outing for them. We also allowed horses to be in hand or ridden. As many people would bring their horses in hand as there would be riding. The other thing we did is make sure that all the obstacles we built or had available were extremely safe. Other people tried to emulate what we did, but they tried to do it in a cheap way and the feedback we got again and again was how fantastic the obstacles were because of how solid and safe they were. People won't come back if they feel there is a high chance their horse could get injured.

Pro's

- Creating the Horse Adventure Park allowed me to use the obstacles for all my Horsemanship courses that I ran – so the Park had multiple uses
- The Park also became a great advertisement for me as an instructor, because people would come along to one of the sessions, meet me and then want to have lessons with me
- The Park was a great way to meet people
- The Park was fantastic for building the confidence of the horses I had in training
- We didn't have to very much to create the Park, we just utilised the facilities we already had and then just added a couple of extra things and it became a huge success
- Initially we had a lot of temporary obstacles and slowly over time as we got more income from the Park we added more permanent obstacles which anyone can do

Con's

- You need to ensure everyone stays safe – we did this by clearly outlining the Health and Safety requirements of those using the park both upon registration to attend and then when we checked everyone in at the beginning of each session
- Again to keep everyone safe you need to monitor the behaviour of the people who come to use the park to ensure

everyone stayed safe. We would speak to anyone who was doing anything we deemed to be unsafe
- People want to pull out at the last minute and get their money back. We made the fee non-refundable because we initially had too many people that wanted to pull out at the last minute when we couldn't fill their space. That fixed the problem and interesting didn't stop anyone booking in.
- You absolutely have to make sure you have to right insurances to cover you and your property in the event that someone or their horse gets injured

WHAT YOU NEED TO GET STARTED AND BE ABLE TO DO THIS

A property that is suitable to use or one that has the potential to create into something that could be used as a Horse Adventure Park.

The correct insurance and liability release form to ensure you cannot be held liable if someone or their horse does get injured.

Suitable health and safety regulations and stipulations and plans on how you will enforce these.

We created a range of obstacles and then advertised our first day on local social media sites. From the beginning we had no problem filling the sessions.

We used Eventbrite event booking software to manage our bookings. You can do it manually or use Eventbrite or something similar.

Horse Gear Hire/Lease/Hire horse Floats/trailers

WHAT IS IT?

This service is about providing equestrian equipment, gear used for horses and Horse Trailers for hire or lease. We started an Equestrian Horse Gear Hire business some years ago and found this to be a very successful business particularly for what I refer to as 'Big ticket' items. What I mean here is items that require a large initial cash outlay such as a horse trailer or a foaling alarm. Horse people who can't afford to purchase these items will often hire or lease them. Smaller priced items such as saddles, helmets, riding Jackets are nowhere near as popular as the big ticket items.

The difference between hire and lease is the length of time. Hire is normally for short periods of time and the costs are higher e.g. days or weeks and lease is normally for items that hired for longer periods of time with the weekly costs being much lower e.g. months or years.

The market is definitely growing for Lease horse floats/trailers. Lots of horse folks can't afford NZ$10,000-NZ$20,000 (GBP£5,000-£10,000/US$6,000-$12,000) to purchase a decent horse trailer, but they can afford to lease one for sometimes years at $100 (GBP£50/US$60) per week. This service generally provides a very good return on investment for those who offer this service.

POTENTIAL INCOME

Depending on what equipment you have available for hire or lease, will dictate how much can be earned but to give you an example:

1. Foaling alarms hire for around NZ$10 (GBP£5/US$6) per day or NZ$70 (GBP£34/US$42) per week – these are generally hired from end of July to February pretty consistently. Total 5 months (153 days) x NZ$10 per day = up to NZ$1,530 (GBP£748/US$915) per season. A foaling alarm costs between AUS$489-$595 and they last for years, that is a very good return on investment

2. Horse floats/Trailer daily for Hire – the average cost of hiring a horse float/Trailer is NZ$70-$100 per day. When we were offering hire floats we were hiring out two floats most weekends and some days during the week. So total income for one float hired at this frequency = 52 weeks of 3 days per week usage = 156 days x NZ$85 day (average) = NZ$13,260 (GBP£6,483/US$8,000) – you can see it doesn't take too long to realise this is a good return on investment – Note we always had good quality horse floats/trailers available for hire, as horse people are quite fussy and generally won't hire anything they think is possibly dangerous or poor quality.
3. Lease Horse Floats/Hire – generally the average cost for a lease horse float/trailer is NZ$100 (GBP£50/US$60) per week. This is a lot less than you can return for hiring out a horse float/trailer but it also requires a lot less input from you, both in time and organisation and generally the horse floats/trailers incur a lot less ware and tear because the same person is using them instead of a different person/horse every day. If a lease horse float/trailer is hired out an average of 40 weeks of the year = 40 x NZ$100 = NZ$4,000 (GBP£2,000/US$2,4000) per year. As I said with this option you don't have to do a lot of work, you just get an income.

Remember I haven't included the costs here that you are responsible for which include insurance, registration or warrant of finesses (if your country has this requirement) that you are responsible for paying for which needs to come off the income.

Pro's

- You can work this around other services you offer
- The need for this service is increasing
- This can be a great earner if you have a horse float/trailer or Equestrian equipment you are not using regularly – that is how

we started this business, we just started hiring equipment and a horse float/trailer we weren't using

Con's

- You need to have a clear agreement the hirers/leasees sign prior to taking the equipment to ensure they pay and what happens if the gear/equipment is damaged. We had someone return the horse float/trailer with a shredded tyre and they didn't want to pay to have it replaced even though they admitted to driving on it for half an hour when it was flat. Fortunately our agreement clearly stated any damage other than normal wear and tear was the responsibility of the hirer
- Ensure you receive payment in advance as it can be impossible to get payment after the hire has taken place
- Ensure you have the correct insurances for whatever you are hiring/leasing as some horses can cause a lot of damage in a very short space of time and if the hirer doesn't have the capacity to pay for the damage, you may need to claim on your insurance
- Ensure you have a way of working around people who book equipment and then don't turn up to take and pay for it. We had this numerous times especially for foaling alarms. They would book them in advance and then not turn up and we would loose potential income.
- You need to check each piece of equipment when it returns from a hire/lease. If you don't you may miss seeing damage that has occurred during the hire that some devious people won't tell you about.

WHAT YOU NEED TO GET STARTED AND BE ABLE TO DO THIS

When we did this, we created a possible hire agreement and got it checked by our lawyer and then advertised locally and almost immediately we were inundated with requests for hires.

Again advertising on local social media is a great way to get this business started. We didn't initially have a website when we started this business but did as went further along. It may be a useful addition but not necessary initially. And again ensure you have the correct insurances to cover you for all eventualities if your equipment/horse float/trailer is involved in some sort of accident.

Horse Trekking/Guided Rides

WHAT IS IT?

This is where you provide the ability for members of the public to come along and ride your horses in interesting and varied surroundings and ideally in beautiful settings.

Horse Trekking can be found in just about every country in the world. Horse Trekking or Guided Rides allow people who like horses but don't own one, to be able to ride a horse. Interestingly many horse owners also do Horse Trekking in order to see different places doing something they love. I have done many horse treks and always enjoy them. Horse Treks or Guided rides can last from ½ hour to weeks long.

POTENTIAL INCOME

This is an interesting one because how much you can earn doing this has so many variables. Firstly you have to own and care for the horses used on the treks which can be costly. Secondly you have to have somewhere to ride. If you have to pay for the 'Somewhere to ride' that cost has to come off what you make. It also depends a lot on how big or small your operation is, how many horses you have and use for the Trekking, how many guides you have or if you do it yourself, if you cater food and provide accommodation for longer rides. The list on this one goes on and on.

If you do this yourself and only have a couple of horses that you use for other things, then it can be all profit. It also dependant on if you do this full time, offering multiple rides a day or just one ride once a week. Costs for Horse Trekking range from NZ$45 (GBP£22/US$27) for 20 minutes for a short pony ride up to NZ$6,300 (GBP£3,000/US$3,800) for 10 day experience per person.

So although I can't give you specifics on this one, it is one you need to do your homework on if you are going to go down this track. It is also vitally important with this option to consider the Health and Safety implications. Horses have a habit of being unpredictable which means people fall off and hurt themselves. When this happens, you need to make sure you have make every possible effort to ensure the people were as safe as they could be, the horses were as well trained as they could be and every effort was made to ensure no one would get hurt. Also for this option you need to make sure you have the correct public liability insurance in place, because if someone does fall off and get hurt, you do not want to be facing a law suite or similar.

PRO'S
- You get to ride a lot
- You get to meet some very interesting people
- Your horses potentially can get lots of riding

CON'S
- There is a higher risk of injury to your customers and you need to be prepared for that, both insurance wise and also by having property trained horses
- You absolutely have to do a lot of homework before embarking on this option – it is not for the faint hearted as people won't ride or treat your horses the way you do and you have to be ok with that
- You need to have good facilities – if your facilities are not good, it sends messages that your whole operation is 'shoddy' and tends not to bring customers back
- There can be considerable outlay on horses, tack and equipment – I know one trekking stable that had to replace the horse covers for its 70 horses which cost them over ten thousand dollars just for the covers!

WHAT YOU NEED TO GET STARTED AND BE ABLE TO DO THIS

Enough suitable quiet well-trained horses and tack to run it. Remembering that a single horse cannot go out on ride after ride after ride. They need rest time and eating time.

A place to ride. Correct insurance. A website advertising what you do, ideally with an automatic booking system.

Hosting visiting Instructors/Clinicians

WHAT IS IT?
If you have the facilities to do this, this can be a very lucrative business. This is where you host different Instructors/Clinicians to come and give lessons and/or clinics at your facilities. You will need to organise and host the instructor/clinician, advertise and organise for people to do lessons and clinics with them and then receive payment from the participants and pay the clinician. This sometimes also involved organising the travel for the Instructor. There are so many different disciplines that you can cover with this, which means you can tap into a wide client base which in turn is a fantastic way of promoting everything you do (other services you offer) as well as your facility.

POTENTIAL INCOME
I know one Equestrian Centre that started doing this and went from having one outside Instructor every now and then to having two or three every week. Sometimes they were there for a couple of hours, sometimes they were there for up to a week giving lessons or a clinic. This Equestrian Centre worked out the total cost to get each instructor there (for local instructors this was nil) including their charges (some instructors charge a per day rate and others charge a per lesson rate) plus any travel costs and then divided that amount by the number of possible lessons. They then added on a margin to each lesson. Lesson costs ranged from NZ$40 (GBP£20/US$24) each for a group of 3-4 riders up to NZ$150 (GBP£73/US$90) per person per 45mins or per hour for other instructors. Effectively every lesson delivered the Equestrian Centre got a cut. Some Instructors were delivering 8-10 lessons a day with the Equestrian Centre making NZ$10-$30 (GBP£5-£15/US$6-$18) per lesson over and above costs. This equals NZ$80-$300 (GBP£40-£150/US$48-$180) day.
The other thing that came out of doing this was that many of the clients who came for lessons with outside instructors wanted to hire

the arenas and attended the other events the Equestrian Centre offered such as Young Rider Show Jumping Competitions, Dressage and Jumping Combined Training competitions and Primary School Show Jumping Competitions. This Equestrian Centre was a roaring success.

PRO'S

- This is a great way to earn money off the facilities that you have and build up a great client database
- You get to meet interesting people
- You get access to a range of instructors that you wouldn't normally have access to to improve your riding
- As mentioned above this is a great way to advertise any other services you offer
- Because you can offer instructors across a wide range of Equestrian disciplines, you are able to tap into a wider client base
- There is almost always a market for this

CON'S

- Sometimes trying to organise people to come along a specific time for lessons can be difficult. The phrase trying to 'herd cats' comes to mind. But if you are clear from the outset that the lessons have to be paid for at the time of booking and they are non refundable, that tends to reduce the number of cancellations and changes you need to do
- Often people don't clean up after themselves (you need to be very specific about this) which means you often have to clean up after people
- You may not like the way people are treating the horses that are using your facilities
- There will be other people on your property

WHAT YOU NEED TO GET STARTED AND BE ABLE TO DO THIS

Firstly you need to have the correct insurances to cover this particularly public liability.

Secondly you need to find a or some instructors who are willing to come to your facility and teach. I haven't found this difficult. Ask questions on social media about who people recommend for lessons on Dressage or Jumping or Horsemanship and then see if they want to come to your property and deliver lessons. Again I have found that instructors generally much prefer to give a bunch of lessons all at once rather than one here and one there. Make sure you find out all their charges before embarking on this.

Have a plan as to how you are going to do bookings. There are online booking sites that can do the bookings such as EventBrite. I have used this site many times and it is fantastic. After you get your event set up, they do the rest for you and then a few days after the event you receive payment minus a small fee. This site was worth its weight in gold and took all of the stress out of organising and taking payment for things like this.

Initially advertising on social media is a good way to start but after you have had a few instructors through, word of mouth will help immensely as well as the fact that everyone who comes and has a lesson, you now have their email address on your database to email with the next lot lessons available.

Judging

WHAT IS IT?
This is where you qualify and become a judge and then you are paid to judge. This works the same for either a breed specific judge or a discipline specific judge. Although this does not tend to be a big income earner, it does allow you to spend a lot of time with lots of horses and potentially travel all over the world.

Becoming a judge is also an excellent way to improve your own ability in any discipline or breed.

Once you qualify as a judge you will be placed on the breed societies qualified judges list or the Equestrian discipline specific qualified judges list. This list contains your contact details and when a show or event is looking for a judge, they go to that list and get in contact.

POTENTIAL INCOME
Generally judges are paid between NZ$100-$350 (GBP£50-170/US$60-$210) per day to judge depending on the breed and discipline. They also normally have their travel, food and accommodation paid for.

As I mentioned above, this is not a huge money making option, but it does have numerous other positives. You learn a lot becoming a judge about a discipline or breed as well as having the opportunity to spend time with other judges.

PRO'S
- This is another great 'Add on' to anything you are already doing particularly if the other options/services you are offering tie you up during the week, this is a great weekend option
- You get to spend heaps of time looking at and often interacting with horses and horse owners
- This is something you can work around your other commitments

- This is a great way to improve any discipline – by becoming a judge you greatly increase your knowledge of what you are trying to achieve within that discipline

Con's
- The days can be long
- You need to be careful when putting ribbons around horses necks as they can be very unpredictable with a flappy, unusual ribbon if they are not used to it
- You can witness people treating their horses cruelly and you may be called upon to disqualify them. Many people don't think they are doing anything wrong with the way they treat their horse. This can be difficult but normally you are taught how to deal with this when you learn to become a judge
- People don't always like how you judge them and can be very rude – always remember that is their issue not yours

What you need to get started and be able to do this
You will need to contact the National breed society or National Equestrian discipline governing body to find out what the criteria and requirements are to become a judge and then you will need to undertake the training and study to complete the required qualifications.

Kids Fun Pony Holiday Camps

WHAT IS IT?
Many riding schools, trekking centres and instructors offer these camps. They bring a group of children together often ranging in ages and skills sometimes with their own ponies and sometimes they are provided by the facility, where the children are given lessons individually and in groups, learn all manner of things about horses everything from how to catch one through to how to clip, they have organised games, sometimes swim if a swimming pool is available and basically are cared for and entertained for a number of days or a week. The children often go for supervised treks as part of this. These camps are normally live in and include meals. These have been become incredibly popular as working parents look for ways to entertain their kids while they are at work.

POTENTIAL INCOME
The average cost of the camps is around NZ$450 (GBP£220/US$270) per child for 3-5 day camps. The numbers on these camps range from 6 – 100. So a potential income of NZ$2,700 (GBP£1,320/US$1,625) up to NZ$45,000 (GBP£22,000/US$27,000) less expenses.

The big thing here is again the ability to fill the participant places. It also requires you to have a facility that has the ability to accommodate and feed this number of children. So again, although this is very good income for a short period of time, it does have some logistical considerations. I know a number of venues that could cater for this number of children with the facilities to run a great camp, so if you look around I am sure you could find something similar. Some of these camps the children bring their own horses and sometimes they use the horses owned by the person offering the camp.

Note again you need to make sure you have the correct public liability insurance in place to cover an event like this, because if someone does get hurt, you do not want to be facing a law suite or similar.

PRO'S
- This type of event can produce a significant amount of income
- These camps can be great fun

CON'S
- You need a special set of skills to run camps for children, in order to keep them all happy and entertained for the full duration of camp
- There is a huge amount of work organising an event like this – venue, food, catering, program, lesson organisation (groups or individual), organising speakers if you are having speakers, planning and preparing demonstrations, first aid provisions can take considerable skill and effort etc etc etc
- You need to have good facilities – Good facilities make running something like this a lot easier as you already have sufficient yards and accommodation so you are not trying to temporarily set up something and then having to take it all down after the event which is a lot more work. You have to be able to house/accommodate the number of ponies and kids involved
- You have to be able to structure a program that will keep all of the children entertained and involved for the whole time

WHAT YOU NEED TO GET STARTED AND BE ABLE TO DO THIS

There are four main things required to get this type of event underway – suitable venue, insurances to cover any possible liability if someone gets hurt, enough suitably qualified instructors/leaders and enough potential participants. Once you have found a suitable venue generating enough children for the event to go ahead is the biggest difficulty. Again a great drawcard to can really help here such e.g. a talk from famous person, or a ride on your best horse or a great prizes or something they can't get anywhere else then you stand a good chance of getting enough participants to make this a huge success.

Structuring a great program will also help. Ideally ensuring you include a combination of individual lessons, group lessons, demonstrations, talks, fun activities including relaxed rides outs, playing with obstacles if you have them available (kids love playing with obstacles). Effectively a great combination of education and entertainment.

Kids Riding Lessons

WHAT IS IT?
This differs from Adult riding lessons in that children can require quite a different skillset. You need to like children and know how to keep them interested and involved during the lesson which can be very different from teaching adults.

Some people love teaching kids and some people don't. Children have a much shorter attention span and tend to get bored quickly if you ask them to repeat something over and over again which isn't wrong, it just requires a different approach. I am constantly being contacted by parents looking for someone to give their children riding lessons. Many parents, when they have children that have an interest in horses/ponies are happy to pay significant sums of money on lessons, if it means they can get away without actually purchasing a pony for the child. This saves them having to worry about who is caring for the pony and where it will be kept to name just a couple of logistical issues that go with ownership. Also if it is just a short phase the child is going through, it is far better to get a few lessons than the outlay for a pony if it is only going to be shortlived.

And apart from that, it's a great way for a child to spend sometime with a horse or pony and find out if they do really like them. Most of the time these lessons are conducted on your ponies/horses. So in order to do this, you will need to have horses or ponies suitable for children to use.

These lesson often also normally include lessons on how to care for the pony as well as how to ride it.

POTENTIAL INCOME
The average cost of children's riding lessons in New Zealand ranges from NZ$35 (GBP£17/US$21) for a pony ride where the child is lead around up to NZ$85 (GBP£42/US$51) for a private lesson.

Again, depending on how many lessons you give per week you can give and how many horses/ponies you have available will determine how much you can earn, as well as the cost of keeping the ponies/horses, has to come off the income produced from the lessons.

Pro's
- It can be a lot of fun helping children improve
- You have flexibility as to when you work
- There is a big call for people wanting riding lessons for children
- If you do this, you can also run School Holiday riding camps as you will already have the ponies and the children

Con's
- If you don't enjoy working with children, this option is for you
- You need to find really good solid ponies that are suitable for children to ride
- This is a very active type of income in that it requires to you to do it in order to make any money and you don't get paid when you are sick
- You need enough space to keep the ponies and you need the facilities such as an arena and toilet facilities if you are going to do this

What you need to get started and be able to do this

You will need to have enough suitable ponies to run this. I know a number of people who started out doing this with just a couple of nice ponies and built their business up to quite a number over a few years.

You will also need to have suitable facilities to be able to do this. You don't necessarily need an arena as I know one lady who ran this in a small paddock where she mowed lanes for the children to follow, but an arena does mean you are less likely to have to cancel lessons due to the footing. You will also need to ensure the children and their families have access to a toilet.

A great website will also help immensely with advertising as parents are always googling riding lessons. There are also lots of social media groups you can advertise your services on as well as advertising in your local supermarket. Many of these ways to advertise are free which really helps.

Make Horse Sales Videos

WHAT IS IT?
Many people have horses to sell but many of them don't know the best way to sell their horse. I have found again and again that horses sell quickly if you can record a video of them ideally doing what they are good at as well as adding in the tasks that everyone wants to see a horse complete such as having its feet picked up, loading into a horse float/trailer or being led. With a video you also have the ability to add in detailed information about the horses pedigree and what they have done in the past/experience they have got.

This option is about creating these videos for people/clients. I have done this and know a number of other people who have also been paid to do this for clients.

If you can record a video and have video editing skills, this is a great option to add to your services list.

POTENTIAL INCOME
These videos can cost anything from NZ$100 (GBP£50/US$60) per horse depending on how fancy/creative you get.

After taking the video of the horse (which the client can do if you are specific about what you want, I can normally create a good quality sales video in a couple of hours.

What you can make from this is again dependant on how many clients want you to do this for them. I find stud farms are a great place to start for clients because they often breed so many horses that they are always looking for ways to advertise and sell them.

I have a very specific set of tasks I like to see on a sales video including the horses movement when it is free in a paddock or arena (ideally walk, trot and small amount of canter), the horse being led towards and away from the camera, the horse standing to have its feet picked out, the horse loading on a trailer, the horse being ridden in the walk, trot and canter both directions and anything else the horse is good at e.g. jumping. BUT the key with the video is to keep it as short as possible. Ideally no more than 6 mins as studies have shown people don't normally watch anything longer than 6 minutes unless they are really interested. There are not very many people doing this currently so this is definitely a niche market that can be tapped into.

Pro's

- You can do this at any time/flexibility on when and how you can do this
- There are not many people offering this service
- Often you will get repeat business from a breeding stud if that is one of your customers

Con's

- It can be time consuming recording the video if you are not clear with the person who owns the horse exactly what you are after
- You need to be careful of any liability issues if the owner makes false claims about the horse and your details appear on the video

WHAT YOU NEED TO GET STARTED AND BE ABLE TO DO THIS

You will need good quality video editing software. I have found a number of pretty cheap options on the internet that work really well. You will need the ability to video the horses. I generally just use my iPhone which works perfectly. You need to advertise and find clients. There are lots of place you can do this, including on social media horse groups as well as contacting horse breeding studs directly. Breed societies often have the heaps of studs contact details on their website which is a great place to start.

I normally publish the videos to YouTube and then send the customer the YouTube link.

Nightshow Performances

WHAT IS IT?
This is performing with your horse(s) in front of crowds of people at Equine Entertainment and Equestrian events. The thing to note here about this option, is this is NOT a demonstration of what you can do with your horse (education), it is a choreographed routine designed to entertain. There are very few people that can do this. When equine events run Entertainment/Educational events such as Equitana in Australia and the USA, Equidays/Equifest in New Zealand, Western States Horse Expo (USA), Del Mar National Horse Show (Night of the Horse) (and there are a huge range of these events in the UK and Europe as well as other countries around the world) they need people who can entertain their crowd in the night shows.

In order to do this you need to have an act or performance. What's an act/performance, an act or performance is something that you and your horse or horses can perform successfully in front of a large crowd. Coming up with an act/performance is often the difficult part. If you google 'great horse acts' you can find a few. You can also google Jean-Francios Pignon or Ben Atkinson and find more but the key is coming up with something that is entertaining and that you and your horse can do successfully in front of a crowd of people. This can take time to create and master and also to get your horse or horses used to large groups of people. The organisers of these shows have great difficulty finding good horse acts/performers, so there is definitely an opportunity here if you are interested in performing.

POTENTIAL INCOME
How much you can earn from this can be dependent on your level of skill, the number of horses you use and how entertaining you are.
Payment for this ranges from NZ$400 (GBP£200/US$240) per performance upwards into the many thousands of dollars.

Pro's
- You get paid to do something that is enjoyable
- You get to attend events and see things that other people don't necessarily get to do and normally for free as you are an exhibitor
- You get to perform with your horse

Con's
- It takes a huge amount of work to create a great performance
- You need to acclimatise your horse to large crowds of people which isn't always easy to do, as where do you get a large crowd that you can take your horse in front of?
- The pay isn't great for the amount of work you have to put in
- When it goes badly, you look and feel like an idiot ☹ and sometimes that happens

What you need to get started and be able to do this

An 'Act/performance' that you can successfully do anywhere. If you can have a couple of horses that are capable of performing, that is even better as if one horse goes lame, you can still use the other one.

You need to get in contact with the event organisers of the events you would like to do a nightshow in and find out what they want and are looking for as the lengths of the performance, the content and exactly the type of performances they are looking for, can differ from event to event. Once you know this you can start to work on creating an act/performance and putting something together that they actually want.

Online Video Courses

WHAT IS IT?
Online Video Courses have become very popular over the last few years particularly since the Pandemic made it impossible for most Horse Trainers/Instructors to make any money at all without having some sort of Online presence. These courses take all sorts of forms. Some trainers have entire libraries or vaults which contain huge quantities of videos, where generally the students pays a monthly fee to watch any or all of the videos. Other trainers have stand-alone courses that they sell individually. Some of these courses have printable notes attached and some are just video courses by themselves. There is a huge range available.

POTENTIAL INCOME
The potential income of the options varies astronomically. I know one US Instructor who has thousands of students paying from US$20 (GBP£21/NZ$33) each per month to part of an online club, which has a huge library of video content. This club also has other advantages such as webinars, equipment and discounted attendance at any of the in person courses. This is a lot of income BUT this club also has a huge digital platform with considerable information technology support to back it up.

I know another US instructor who won't take anyone on his clinics unless they are a member of his online video 'club' which costs US$29 per month and again has a huge vault of videos and information. I don't know how many members he has, but believe it is quite a few.

Another instructor has a video classroom which contains hundreds of videos and has a US$29 (GBP£24/NZ$48) monthly subscription fee. Again I do know how many students this instructor has but understand it is quite a few.

Each of the above instructors have invested considerable sums of money into developing their online capabilities and presence. This does come at a cost as you have to either have access to or employ specialist Information and Technology staff. Other smaller scale options exist where you can build an online learning library using any one the numerous web-based platforms such as Thinkific. They provide the platform and all you do is load your videos up onto. These products allow you to build, grow and sell your online courses and prices start at $39 USD per month. You can also just advertise your courses on social media for sale with your contact details. The customers then pay you via PayPal or online banking and you email them the link to the video(s). There are heaps of different ways to do this. This is a great way to test the market and see if what you have for sale (topics/videos) is marketable.

So the potential income from this is significant particularly if you already have a client base.

PRO'S

- You are not limited to local – courses can be purchased by anyone from anywhere in the world
- The number of courses you sell is not limited by your time – as basically you create it once and then sell it over and over again
- If you have knowledge on a particular subject this is a great way to be able to sell it to lots of people
- It is possible to make significant sums of money doing this

CON'S

- This requires some Information Technology skills
- You need to have someone who can video you or purchase the likes of a PIVO that allows you to video yourself
- You need video editing software and the skills to use it – but they aren't difficult to learn to use and there are a number of free video editing software packages available

WHAT YOU NEED TO GET STARTED AND BE ABLE TO DO THIS

A product – basically you need to plan out what you want to make a video course of.

The ability to record video – a simple smartphone works, you just need someone to video you or have access to the likes of a PIVO which turns your smartphone into a personal cameraman. As listed above – there are a myriad of ways to sell online video courses once you have recorded them. You will also need to advertise the courses you have available for sale, which you can do at no cost on social media.

Photographing Horses

WHAT IS IT?
This is where you either go to horse shows or horse events and take photos of the horses there and then sell them to their owners or you visit horse studs and take photos of their horses, that the breeders can then use to advertise and sell their horses or where you take portrait type photos of horses with their owners for a fee or you do a combination of all three.

If you love photography and you love horses, then this could be the option for you. Horse owners LOVE to have great photos of them doing things with their beloved horses. Horse owners are generally very open to purchasing great photos of their horses especially they themselves are in the photos too.

As I mentioned above there are three basic categories that equine photography falls into.

1. Going to horse shows or events and taking photos and then selling the photos to the owners. Horse show and event organisers really struggle to get photographers who are keen to undertake this, as it requires some effort following the event sorting out the good photos from the bad and selling them to the owners.
2. Contracting to Horse Studs/breeders to visit their property and photograph the horses they require
3. Doing portrait style photos for individuals – the best way to do this, is do this for a group of people such as at a Pony Club Camp where you can photograph 30 children one after the other or at a clinic where there a number of people keen to have this done, all in one place.

POTENTIAL INCOME
There are lots of options for how this can work. For option 1 above, I know a number of photographers who sell per photo. The prices range

from NZ$5 - NZ$20 (GBP£2.50-£10/US$3-$12) per photo. When you have taken photos of between 1-200 horses this can be a significant income. If half of the horse owners brought 1 photo at NZ$10 (GBP£5/US$6) each = NZ$100 x NZ$10 (Avg) = NZ$1,000 (GBP£500/US$600) per show/event. You can offer the digital print which is what most people want or a physical print at a higher cost. I know a number of photographers who do this every weekend and do extremely well out of it.

For option 2 above, there are multiple ways to do this. I have been charged NZ$10 (GBP£5/US$6) per photo that I like as well as being charged a daily rate of NZ$500 (GBP£244/US$300) (Avg) and then I can all the photos taken during the day and I can pick and choose between which ones I use and which ones I don't. The good thing about this option is you can take as many photos as you want and every conceivable angle and it doesn't cost you or the breeder any more. Many breeders like this option. If you did this for 10 studs x NZ$500 = NZ$5,000 (GBP£2,445/US$3,000).

For option 3 above, I know a number of photographers who do this and they generally charge a set fee of between NZ$100 - NZ$300 (GBP£60-£146/US$48-$180). For the set fee you get 5 different photographs of yourself with your horse and in some cases they are physical printed photos as well as the digital prints that the individual can then use however they want. If you can do this with 10 children/adults in one sitting = NZ$200 (Avg) x 10 = NZ$2,000 (GBP£1,000/US$1,200).

PRO'S

- This is another great 'Add on' to anything you are already doing particularly if the other options/services you are offering tie you up during the week, this is a great weekend option
- For the time invested it is a great little income earner
- You get to spend heaps of time with horses and horse owners

- This is something you can work around your other commitments

Con's

- You need a good camera, if you don't already have one - in saying that I purchased an excellent digital camera with a great zoom lense for around NZ$500 (GBP£245/US$300) on special. It takes excellent photos particularly of horses because it has a 'sports' setting which speeds up the shutter speed to ensure I don't get blurry photos when they horses move
- You need to find people who want this service – but I see horse shows and events advertising for these services all the time, so I know there is a demand
- Not all horses are easy to get a great photo of because they won't put their ears forward or the weather that day is terrible which makes taking great photos really hard. Luckily that is the exception not the norm.

What you need to get started and be able to do this

You will need a good camera. But as I mentioned above, you can now purchase a great digital camera at a very reasonable price. My wonderful husband actually purchased mine for me for Christmas which was a real bonus.

You need to find people who want your services, but advertising on local equine focused social media can really drum up some business in this area. Google breed societies, who normally advertise all the big stud farms and contact them directly offering your service. Google horse events or if you don't know what events are coming up, ask on local chat forums which are the big horse events in your area and then get in contact with the organisers. If you offer to take their photos, you are removing one more thing they have to organise and they will love you for it!

Make sure you have the right insurances for this. And beware about just turning up at a show and photographing horses and then trying to sell directly to the owners. You need to make sure you have permission before doing this.

Picking Up Manure

WHAT IS IT?

Everywhere there are horses, there is horse manure that needs to be picked up. Effectively horse manure either needs to be picked up and removed from a horses paddock or the owner of the horse needs the ability to shift the horse out of the paddock once there is too much manure for it to continue to live there and then harrow it (spread the manure). The reason for this is that if the horses eat grass surrounding their manure they pick up parasites living in and around the manure which are bad for the horses. A heavy parasite infestation in a horse can be fatal. More than 50% of horse owners pickup and remove the manure from their horses paddocks. Many horse owners don't like this job and are very willing to pay someone else to do it. I have paid people to pick up manure for me many many times and know many other horse owners who do the same.

A number of the young people I have paid to pick up manure for me, have also done other work for me including grooming, feeding and caring for my horses. I have taught a number of them horsemanship and they have then gone on to do other things within the horse industry. This is an entry level position in the horse industry but one there is always call for and one that allows you to work with and around horses.

It is also one that allows you to learn from the owners of the horses if you are keen to learn more.

There are lots of way to pick up horse manure. It can be picked up using a shovel and wheel borrow, a fork and a wheel barrow, by hand using rubber gloves and a bucket or using machinery such as a Horse Manure Vacuum or a motorised Horse Manure collection device that tend to use a brushing motion which are both towed behind a quad bike.

Potential Income

The hourly rate for this tends to be minimum wage. In New Zealand that is currently between NZ$17-NZ$21 (GBP£8-£10/US$10-$12) per hour. I usually paid my staff 6-10 hours per week, I generally always allowed a little extra time so that they could groom all of my horses as well. This meant that these staff got some enjoyable horse time as well as the more physically demanding horse manure picking up.

Total Income using an average 8 hours x NZ$20 (GBP£10/US$12) per hour = NZ$160 (GBP£78/US$96) per week. And that was just working for me. If you pick up manure for a few horse owners each week, this can add up.

Pro's

- There are always horse owners looking for someone to pick up manure – so there is always a need for this option
- You get to spend time around horses
- This is an excellent way to keep physically fit and healthy
- As there was with the staff that worked for me picking up manure, they got to do other things with my horses and learn horsemanship skills from me in the process. A couple of the staff who worked for me came to horse shows with me and learnt about showing, about show preparation and about handling the horses at a show which tends to be more stressful for a horse than when they are at home
- If you are good worker, this is a great way to get a start working in the horse world

Con's

- This has to be done in all weathers, as the horses keep passing manure, it must be picked up
- This is not a glamours job

- Some horses are experts at tipping wheel barrows over which they particularly love to do when they are full of manure. That can be exasperating.

WHAT YOU NEED TO GET STARTED AND BE ABLE TO DO THIS
You need to be reliable and willing to work in all weathers. You can advertise that you are looking for this type of role on any local equestrian social media site. You can just walk into any property that has horses and offer to work there. I have had a number of people walk in off the street and offer to do this and I have hired them on the spot for there tenacity and willingness to come in and ask.

Pony Club (4H) Instructors – note this differs from being a Clinician (as generally this is for one on one lessons) and giving riding lessons (as you don't have to provide horses)

What is it?
Pony Clubs are always looking for Instructors. Although these are generally not paid positions, it does give you the opportunity to gain skills by learning how to teach, understand the Pony club curriculum and build up clients, as many of the children often become clients.

I know one Pony Club instructor who teaches at Pony Club for free every other weekend and then gives heaps of chargeable lessons outside of Pony Club as well as running kids camps in the school holidays with the same children (and many others) that she does very well financially out of.

Pony Clubs have a set curriculum which the members work through with the assistance of their instructors. This curriculum is basic but definitely teaches you lots. There is also lots of support in place in the Pony Club system to help improve/educate the instructors.

Potential Income
I know one Pony Club instructor who charges NZ$40-NZ$65 (GBP£20-£31/US$24-$39) (price varies depending on the topic and the individual wanting the lessons e.g. Child or Adult, Beginner or Advanced) for individual one on one lessons as well as running kids camps each school holidays. She does between 5 – 15 lessons a week. Earning between NZ$200 - NZ$750 (GBP£97-£366/US$120-$451) week plus extra from camps in the school holidays.

This instructor also does group lessons on theory needed to sit the various Pony Club certificates.

Becoming a Pony Club instructor is a great way to start out as you can just volunteer to do this and be learning for free from other instructors. It is also a great way to see the problems and issues that riders have and that you need to learn how to deal with.

Pro's

- Pony Clubs are always looking for help so you can generally volunteer at just about any pony club no matter what level of skills you have got
- This is a great way to spend time around horses
- This is a great to learn lots of skills
- This is a great way to get clients
- You will get to teach a lot of different ponies and riders

Con's

- Learning this way can be slow
- It can take a while to build up credibility to the point where riders want to take lessons from you

What you need to get started and be able to do this

You can search on the internet for Pony Clubs near you. They always have the contact details of the head instructor. Get in contact with the head instructor, offer your services/willingness to help and see what is possible. Offer your services and say you are keen to learn. I did this and was welcomed with opened arms.

Most Pony Clubs allow adult members. Become an adult member to find out what the pony club does and when their events are on. Offer to assist an any event they run. This is a great way to get to know the people involved in running the Pony Club.

Pony Parties

WHAT IS IT?
This is where you travel to a customers home with a couple of extremely well behaved ponies and be the entertainment at a child's birthday party, where the children ride and spend time with the ponies.

This can work extremely well if you have ponies with the right temperament for it. They have to be 100% ok with children of all shapes, sizes and noise levels being near them, on them and around them. Then you spend an hour or two giving pony rides as well as supervising the children spending time patting and enjoying the ponies. Some people who do this, also have other farmyard type animals that they can take along such as friendly rabbits and guinea pigs.

POTENTIAL INCOME
The income potential for this option varies greatly depending on how much equipment you have available for sale, what sort of equipment you are selling and where and how you decide to sell it. In my case as I was primarily selling to my students when they needed extra equipment. I earned around NZ$200 (GBP£97/US$120) per month. My friends made between NZ$500-NZ$5,000 (GBP£244-£2,445/US$300-$3,000) per event.

Example One: Mobile Pony Parties
They bring two cute ponies for 1 hour offering lots of pony riding, leading, decorating the pony, brushing & plating, as an added experience we also bring our rabbits and guinea pigs for the children to enjoy. Cost = NZ$300 (GBP£146/US$180) Pony Party + Rabbits & Guinea Pigs, NZ$350 (GBP£171/US$210) Unicorn Pony Party + Rabbits @ Guinea Pigs (1 pony being our colored unicorn pony), NZ$400 (GBP£195/US$240) Pony Party + Rabbits & Guinea Pigs with your

choice of added farmyard friend. Animals available - bottle feed lambs, goat, alpaca, donkey, pig, chickens.

Example Two: Birthday Parties

We come to your event with our beautiful Welsh Ponies and/or Miniature Horses and provide a minimum of one hour of led pony rides. Age group 1 - 10 year olds. Children can do riding, grooming, petting, decorating and feeding the ponies. Cost = 1 x Riding Pony for 1hr NZ$395 (GBP£193/US$237), 2 x ponies for 1hr NZ$595 (GBP£290/US$358).

Example Three: Mini Pony Party – Cost £200 (NZ$408/US$246) – Ages 2-8yrs. For 1 hr and up to 10 children (2 ponies). Includes Fancy dress with riding and grooming.

Example Four: Parties at your property – These can be held in your garden if you have enough space. They pre-visit to ensure health and safety. We can run the party in 2 ways when we come off site. We recommend the mentioned number of children if we are to take the children as our responsibility and run as a normally party, or you can just hire us for this amount of time and have as many children as you wish, making sure you filter them out to us so as not to overwhelm the ponies and we will just continuously offer pony rides. Cost = 1hr £350 (NZ$715/US$430) up to 8 children. 1.5hrs £400 (NZ$817/US$492) up to 10 children. 2hrs £450 (NZ$920/US$554) up to 12 children.

PRO'S

- You can do this most days of the week as well as the weekend
- This can be a great income earner
- This is a great way to spend lots of time around horses and children
- If you already have one or two great ponies, this can be a great way to spend time with them

CON'S

- Children can get hurt around horses and ponies - Safety is your number one concern. You have to make sure the children and ponies are safe at all times and that no one can get hurt
- You have to make sure you have the right insurance to cover you in the event someone did get hurt
- You have to love children
- You have to make sure you have ponies who love kids and don't mind being fussed over
- People can mess you round with bookings especially at busy times of the year – you can help alleviate this by getting a sizeable non-refundable deposit
- If it is pouring with rain, you need have a plan for what you will do as you don't want to have to can and lose money every time it rains

WHAT YOU NEED TO GET STARTED AND BE ABLE TO DO THIS

The most important thing with this option is you must have a couple of fantastic ponies. Ponies that love children and are happy to have children on and around them. If you have access to these type of ponies, you are over half way there. Make sure you have the right insurance to cover you if one of the children did get hurt or if one of your ponies caused damage to someone's property. Ensure you have safe clean equipment you can use on the ponies at a birthday party. Establish how you might run the party so everyone including the ponies remain safe and happy. You will need the ability to transport your ponies to the location of the party. Some of the businesses I found running pony parties, would go out and visit the location of the party prior to taking their ponies there to ensure the location was large enough and they could set it up safely, you may want to do this. Establish how much you are going to charge and how you are going to take bookings. As I mentioned above consider what you will do if it rains. Determine how much you are going to charge and then start advertising. Advertising in local school newsletters are a good place to start.

Pre-School Training

WHAT IS IT?
Horses are generally a lot easier to break in or start under saddle if they have had some training before being started/broken to saddle. Some trainers also offer this service which is done between 18 – 30 months, which sets your horse up really well, so that when they get started under saddle, the whole process is a lot easier for them because they have already had some of the training and understand what is happening. Also if pre school training is done when the horse is around 2 years old, because they are young and still very willing to learn they tend to be a lot more accepting at this age than as a three or four year old when most horses are sent for breaking in/starting under saddle. Pre school training normally takes around 2-3 weeks and often (but not always) covers the following:

To be caught, led, tied up, washed, covered. Also easy for the farrier, vet and other health professionals to work with. Some trainers also teach the horse to be long reined during this training.

POTENTIAL INCOME
How much you can earn from this is dependant on how many horses you get for this type of training as its not a really popular form of training but in saying that it is more prevalent now than it has ever been in the past.

Charges for this are generally a flat fee. Prices I have been quoted for this type of training:

- Trainer 1 - NZ$760 (GBP£371/US$457) flat fee excludes feed but including hay
- Trainer 2 - NZ$1050 (GBP£513/US$632) geldings and fillies flat fee which normally takes 3 weeks – hay and feed is included. Note colts are extra being NZ$1,190 (GBP£581/US$716) for colts

Pro's
- Young horses are generally much easier to teach than older horses more set in their ways, so this training can be very enjoyable and rewarding
- There is a reasonable quick turn around with these horses so you can generate more income

Con's
- This is a relatively new service so you will need to advertise quite a bit that you provide this type of service in order to generate business – but this can be done quite effectively on social media for very low expenditure if any.
- Some young horses have had little or no handling when they arrive so you need to have good facilities to be able to hold the horses while they learn to be caught

What you need to get started and be able to do this
You need to have good general horsemanship skills to be able to do this well. Young horses are generally easy to work with if you have the right skills. It is very important that you are a VERY patient person when working with young horses as you are effectively setting them up for the rest of their lives. If you are aggressive or punish young horses you can ruin them for life. Do not undertake this type of training if you are not patient and really enjoy working with young horses.

You need to have a written contract with the owner of the horse outlining what you aim to achieve with their horses within the timeframe you have the horse.

You will need to have space to be able to care for and keep the horses while you work with them.

Social media is a great place to generate clients for Pre-school training. As I have already outlined you will need to do a bit of advertising to generate business. Don't be scared to write a story on what this is and what you do and send it to local newspapers, they are always looking for stories.

A contract for the owners to sign prior to you taking their horses for pre-school training – I don't have any examples of this, but you can adjust one of the breaking in contracts

Problem Solving

WHAT IS IT?
This involves you either taking a horse(s) and problem solving behavioural issues or where you travel to peoples properties fixing problems for owners who don't have the skills to fix them themselves such as trailer loading issues. I know a number of trainers who have made full time businesses out of doing just this. If you are very good at something like fixing trailer loading issues or jumping issues or go forward issues then this option could be for you.

There are so many issues that many people don't have the skills or ability to solve, where they always looking for someone more skilled to help them. I have been asked to Problem solve a heap of different issues for people. Things like Trailer Loading (as already mentioned, tying up issues, horses not wanting to be clipped, horses who won't stand for the farrier, horses that won't be washed, horses that are extremely herd bound, horses that won't go forward, horses that won't stop, horses that won't be caught. The list of things that people need help with is extensive.

POTENTIAL INCOME
I normally charge between NZ$100-NZ$150 (GBP£48-£73/US$60-$90) per hour rate plus travel costs for these types of fixes and tell people right from the start that it may take multiple sessions to start seeing an improvement. I personally prefer to teach the people what to do to fix the problem rather than just teaching the horse. This way I know that that person will be in a position to deal with the problem should it reoccur when I am not around but some trainers, charge a specific fee and just work on fixing the specific problem with the horse. I know one trainer who charges NZ$350 (GBP£171/US$210) for two hours to fix a trailer loading issue. The problem with this is that you can often get a horse in the trailer inside two hours unless it is a very extreme case, but that doesn't mean the horse is fixed for life. It means the

trainer got the horse in the trailer on this occasion. Often this requires the client to pay this several times in order to make real progress with their horse.

Another trainer I know offers a package deal where you pay for 10 visits and it costs XX amount of dollars, depending on what you are fixing and how extreme the horse is that you are working with. This could be anything from NZ$500 - NZ$5,000 (GBP£244-£2445/US$300-$3010) for the 10 visits.

But one thing is for certain and that is that there is definitely a market for this service in any horsey area.

How much you can make doing this depends on how many clients you can fit in a any week and how many clients you can find who want your services.

Pro's

- This work is very flexible – you can generally organise it around anything else you are doing
- This is a great way to spend time around horses
- This is a great to learn lots of new skills – especially when you encounter a horse that doesn't respond to your solution
- This is a great way to get clients – I have had a number of people who have come to me for this service and ended up coming to clinics I run or take individual lessons from me
- You will get to teach a lot of different horses and ponies

Con's

- It can take a while to build up a client base who want this service
- Some horses won't respond to your way of teaching/fixing the problem and some horses will require a lot more time than you have available – you can mitigate this by offering a money back guarantee

- Some horses can be extremely difficult and even dangerous – you have to be prepared to walk away and give the owner back their money as getting injured would mean you won't be able to work

WHAT YOU NEED TO GET STARTED AND BE ABLE TO DO THIS

You have to have the skills to fix a problem or problems. The good thing about this is you can study so many different options on the internet these days to learn. I know one trainer who offered to fix trailer loading issues for free to the first 50 clients. This gave him lots of time learn and allowed him to gain lots of skills with lots of different horses. It also got his name out there and actually ended up being an incredible marketing exercise.

If you have the skills to do this, next you need to find clients. Again spreading the word via social media is a great option or getting in contact with local riding groups and offering to do a free demonstration or offering your services is also a good option. Make sure you have the right insurances for your country so that you are covered should you or the horse get injured.

Retired Horse Sanctuary/Racehorse spelling

WHAT IS IT?
This option differs from the 'General Horse Grazing/Boarding/Livery Services' option in that normally the horses involved in this option are turned out in groups with other horses of similar personality in larger paddocks and for a longer periods of time/up to years. You as the facility owner look after them and the owner only sees these horses occasionally, if at all.

This option has come about because many people are looking for somewhere suitable for their older horse to retire in comfort and again don't have the time or space to keep them at home themselves. They don't want them sold, they just want them well cared for while they live out their days in piece and quiet.

Race Horse Spelling also falls under this option as often race horses need time off from training or racing and the racing stables don't have the time or space to care for race horses not currently in work, so again pay someone else to do it. Often race horses are turned out with other horses and allowed to just be a horse for a period of time, until they are fit and healthy and ready to go back to racing.

POTENTIAL INCOME
How much you can earn for this depends on how much space you have available and how many horses you have the time to take care of. Because these horses are turned out (not in work), there tends to be a lot less work (your time) involved. If a horse gets injured or requires special care, then they will require more care.

Note:- I have worked the possible incomes on 10 horses. Many of these facilities I found who offer this service accommodate considerably more than 10 horses, but this at least gives you an idea of what is possible.

The Example I found of someone offering this service – pastures range in size from five to 20 acres, varying terrain and trees for shade. Horses are integrated into small herds. Prices start from NZ$80

(GBP£40/US$47) per week for retired horses (includes grazing and hay as needed, hoof care, worming, and photo updates). Horses are checked during the day. Total per year for 10 horses = 10 x NZ$80 (GBP£40/US$47) x 52 = NZ$41,600 (GBP£20,000/US$25,000).

Pro's

- As these horses are generally turned out (in pasture all the time), they tend to require a less work than a full service Liberty stable where the horses are often stabled and then turned out for a portion of the day – generally daily checking and in winter the feeding of hay or supplemental feed. Some older horses do require daily feeding of medications and special feeds.
- If you already have the space and facilities, this can be a good option where you get to work and interact with lots of lovely old gentle horses
- This is a great way to meet lots of people

Con's

- Sometimes owners don't pay their bill, so you need to have strategies in place to ensure you get paid. These could include legal contracts and/or written agreement with the owners prior to accepting their horses
- If a horse you have grazing at your property gets injured, you will need to tend to it and also make sure you have the correct liability and insurances to cover yourself for this eventuality
- When the time comes to put an older horse to sleep due to illness or health issues making its quality of life no longer sustainable, you will need to be there with the vet when this is done. You will also need to arrange for the burial of the horse. This is very difficult for some people. If you find this part of owning a horse extremely difficult, this option may not be for you.

- Owners may want to visit their horses at inconvenient times of the day or weekend – you can stipulate when they can visit in the contract to alleviate issues surrounding this
- Some horses can be difficult to catch and deal with especially if they get injured and require attention from a vet – good horsemanship skills can help immensely with this

WHAT YOU NEED TO GET STARTED AND BE ABLE TO DO THIS

You will need a boarding contact/agreement. I decided not to include a sample boarding contact in this book because every country around the world has different legal requirements. If you do a Google search on horse boarding or grazing for horses in your country, you will be able to find numerous examples of boarding contracts that you can use as a starting point. Another option is to seek the advice of a lawyer on this. They can make sure you are covered legally as well as ensuring you are in a position to be able to collect any unpaid fees. You will also need to ensure you have the ability to put the horse to sleep should the need arise and that the owner is happy to pay these costs as well as the costs to bury the horse.

If you have these services available, it could be worth creating a website and advertising this. You can also advertise on any local equestrian social media sites to get your name out there. Word of mouth normally takes over after a period of time.

Ensure you have the necessary insurances as well as being very clear about what you will and will not do for the horses in your care.

Sale on Behalf

WHAT IS IT?
Selling on Behalf means you take other peoples horses and firstly prepare them for sale and then secondly sell them for the owners.

Many people don't have the time or the inclination to meet potential purchases to sell their horses so they employ other people to sell their horses for them on behalf. For people who are good at dealing with people as well as horses, this could be an excellent income earner. Trainer number 1 that I refer to did this full time and nothing else. She had minimum of a 4 week wait list and was very good and getting horses going well and then selling them

POTENTIAL INCOME
How much you can earn from this is dependant on how many horses and/or ponies you sell and over what time frame. Generally trainers charge a weekly rate to prepare the horse for sale/ride it and get sales photos etc plus hay and feed and then a commission on sale. Trainer 1 below sold approximately 260 horses using this formular over the course of two years. She didn't own her own property, but rented land and still managed to make a very good income using this formular. She would have approximately 5 – 6 horses in at any time. This equates to NZ$50,000-NZ$60,000 (GBP£24,452-£29,343/US$30,107-$36,129) pa less expenses. Trainer 2 does this in conjunction with breaking in horses and producing show jumpers which she competes. Trainer 3 also does this in conjunction with breaking horses in and taking horse for schooling. Note Trainer 3 lives on her Mum and Dads farm and has plenty of space for the horses so she doesn't have to worry about the cost of feed as all their hay is made on the property so is able to discount that off her price.

These are some of charges I have been quoted for this service.
- Trainer 1 - NZ$30 (GBP£14/US$18) per day (NZ$210 (GBP£102/US$126) week) which excludes feed and hay but

Includes outings, sale photos, regular updates, 5-6 sessions per week, advertisment, presenting for buyers etc. No commission on sale.
- Trainer 2 - NZ$250 (GBP£122/US$150) week plus feed/hay – plus take a 10% commission on sale
- Trainer 3 - NZ$200 (GBP£97/US$120) week includes hay – plus take a 10% commission on sale

Pro's
- In any area with a good number of horses, there are always people looking for a good rider to take their horse and sell it on behalf. A good rider can make a mediocre horse look great and therefore make it a lot easier to sell
- There is potentially good money to be earned doing this
- You get the opportunity to ride and work with a huge range of horses

Con's
- Some horses can be difficult to ride and/or work with
- You can get injured by a horse that has underlying behavioural issues
- Some owners want far too much for their horses, but if you ensure they understand they are unlikely to sell if over priced, it doesn't matter as you still get paid per week even if they don't sell

What you need to get started and be able to do this
You need to have good general horsemanship skills as well as knowing where the best place to advertise horses for sale is in your area.
Social media is a great place to generate clients from for Sale on Behalf. Advertise you have availability and to contact you for costs.
Space and the ability to care for the horses while in work

Some trainers have a form they get you to fill in in advance requesting all the information about the horse they want you to sell including any issues or known behavioural issues as well as costs the client agrees to pay. This form is the contact the binds the client to pay you. Creating a form like this is well worthwhile. It does not need to be complex just work out what information you want to know and draw one up. Ensure the client signs the contract PRIOR to taking their horse.

Schooling – like bringing horses back into work or putting miles in the saddle

WHAT IS IT?
Schooling horses and charging for it is one of the most common ways make money from horses. Depending on your area of skill can determine if you have a specific focus for what type of schooling you offer or like many trainers you can just offer generic schooling.

This can be simply putting miles in the saddle for a young horse so they are more confident and easier to ride or it can be bringing horses back into work after they have been turned out or had a foal for example.

Some trainers offer discipline specific schooling such as show training or dressage (flat work) schooling or some trainers even take horses to prepare them for endurance racing. There are lots of options that fall under this heading but it generally covers taking a horse and improving its already existing skills not problem solving behavioural issues which falls under Problem Solving option covered elsewhere in this book.

POTENTIAL INCOME
How much you can earn from this is again dependant on how many horses and/or ponies you can take on at any given time. Generally trainers charge a weekly rate but some trainers charge a full price charge such as, I take your horse for 6 weeks, prepare it of X show and then show it at X show in X number of classes and there is a one off cost for this.

These are some of charges I have been quoted for this service. As you can see Trainer one is significantly more expensive than 2 and 3 but she is also an exceptional rider, with lots of wins in show jumping behind her. Trainers 2 and 3 are more run of the mill in that they both good riders who do this for a living but without any huge success in any specific discipline.

Even if you have only two horses in for schooling at any one time, that is approx. NZ$400 (GBP£195/US$240) per week or NZ$20,000 (GBP£9,781/US$12,043) per year excluding costs.
- Trainer 1 - NZ$350 (GBP£171/US$210) week which excludes feed and hay
- Trainer 2 - NZ$195 (GBP£95/US$117) week includes feed but excludes shoeing and teeth
- Trainer 3 - NZ$200 (GBP£97/US$120) week includes hay

Pro's
- In any area with a good number of horses, there are always people looking for a good rider to take their horse and do some schooling.
- There is potentially good money to be earned doing this especially if you can take a few horses on at any one time.
- Some people just want you to ride their horse and put some milage in the saddle, so effectively you get paid for a ridding a horse! How cool is that!
- You get the opportunity to ride and work with a huge range of horses.

Con's
- Some horses can be difficult, to ride, bring back into work and/or work with in general
- You can get injured by a horse that has underlying behavioural issues
- Some owners want you to perform miracles in a very short time frame – a good way to combat this problem is to take the horse for a week at the owners cost and spend the week doing an evaluation of what you think you can achieve with it in what timeframe. Then present that to the owner. I know a number of trainers who will only take horses for schooling with this

caveat in place. This normally removes the issue of owners wanting miracles.

WHAT YOU NEED TO GET STARTED AND BE ABLE TO DO THIS

You need to be a good confident rider with good problem solving skills. The more of a generalist (can do anything) you are when it comes this, the greater the market you can tap into. For example if you can improve horses flatwork/dressage, their jumping and/or educate a horse for the showring, you will have way more customers than someone who is more narrowly focused like good at improving a horses flat work/dressage.

Social media is a great place to generate clients. Advertise you have availability and to contact you for costs.

Space and the ability to care for the horses while in work

Some trainers have a form they get you to fill in in advance requesting all the information about the horse they want you to school including any issues or known behavioural issues as well as costs the client agrees to pay. This form is the contact the binds the client to pay you. Creating a form like this is well worthwhile. It does not need to be complex just work out what information you want to know and draw one up. Ensure the client signs the contract PRIOR to taking their horse

Sell Horse Manure – Liquid, Powered or Normal

WHAT IS IT?

Everyone who is involved with horses knows that horses produce a lot of manure. If the owners collect the horse manure/remove the horse manure from the paddocks, you have to do something with it. And if you just put it in a pile, the pile tends to grow very quickly. This option is about producing an income by selling this by product that horses already produce.

Most horse owners don't do anything with their horses manure, but if you are prepared to spend some time, this option can be produce a regular income. I had a very good friend that used to make up to NZ$50 a week, selling her horse manure at the gate. She would bag up her horse manure into the feed bags that her horses feed came in and place the bags at her gate with an honesty box. She lived just on the edge of town and as fast as she would place the bags at the gate, they would be sold. The honesty box allowed people to pay without her having to be there.

I have also seen horse manure sold by the trailer load as well as sold powered. When you collect horse manure using a manure vacuum cleaner, like a Greystone Maxivac (that's what we have), it actually breaks up the manure, so it comes out almost powered. Gardener's love this, because it means that the manure breaks down in their garden much quicker than big hard clumps.

I have also seen people soak their horse manure in a muslin cloth, in water, and then sell the manure water. The manure water is full of nutrients that leach out from the manure, but it doesn't produce the weeds which you can get from normal horse manure, if it is not well rotted before being placed on the garden.

POTENTIAL INCOME

The income potential for this option varies depending on where you are located, how many bags you put out for sale each week and if your manure is powered, liquid or bagged.

As I mentioned above a friend of mine would put up around 25 bags of manure each week and sell each bag for NZ$2 (GBP£1/US$1.20) making up to NZ$50 (GBP£24/US$30) per week.

I have seen bottles of manure water sell at fares and fetes for NZ$2-$5 (GBP£1-£2.50/US$1.20-$3) bottle and bags of powered manure sell for up to NZ$5 (GBP£2.50/US$3) a bag. How many bags you put out for sale often determines how much you make.

We have also sold trailer loads of horse manure for NZ$10 (GBP£5/US$6) per trailer load. With this option, the people buying the horse manure shovelled the manure onto their trailer themselves.

Pro's
- The best thing about this option is that it gets rid of your horse manure AND you get money for it
- There is always a ready supply
- You can sell it year round

Con's
- If you live a long way away from a town, it can be difficult to sell unless you take it somewhere such as a local market to sell
- It does require time and work to bag up the manure or soak the manure to make manure water
- If you don't bag it up, you can't sell it
- If you use an honesty box, some people won't pay (will steal the manure), although I have not had that problem at all
- It can be messy to deal with, but nothing that a good pair of rubber gloves can't solve

What you need to get started and be able to do this

Firstly you need some horse manure. Generally anyone with horses will be willing to give you their horse manure to sell, if you don't have enough or any of your own.

Decide where and how you are going to sell it. You may need to source bags. Generally most horse racing stables have feed bags that they are happy to give away, if you ask. You will need a sizeable sign that you can erect somewhere to attract attention to your manure. Bag up your manure and ensure the top of the bags are well fastened. I normally use Binder Twine that comes off hay bales. Tied tightly, it normally works really well. A great place to advertise your manure is on local supermarket noticeboards or on local social media for sale sites.

Selling Horse Themed Giftware

WHAT IS IT?
Horsey people LOVE to buy things with horses on them. Everything from bags to stationery, to blankets to jewellery to coaster and placemats.

This option requires you to find a supplier(s) of different horse themed giftware and then sell it at a profit. When we did this, we went along to the New Zealand gift fair which is held three times a year. There are gift fairs held all over the world. This is where wholesalers go and set up big stalls showing everything they can supply to you/the gift shops around the country. These gift fairs sell all sorts of items including horse themed giftware. We found a heap of different suppliers at the gift fairs who were able to supply us with a great range of horse orientated giftware.

We sold our horse themed giftware in a range of ways. We had a small shop at our property that we opened for a couple of hours once a week as well as attending horse shows, local agricultural shows as well as on the internet. This option does require you to initially outlay some capital to purchase the products you are going to sell.

POTENTIAL INCOME
At every event we attended we sold between NZ$1,000 - NZ$3,000 (GBP£489-£1467/US$602-$1806) depending on the size of the event and what the weather was like. If the weather was beautiful, more people would attend the event and we always sold a lot more. We tried to attend 2 events a month during the spring, summer and autumn. From doing these events alone we were making - 18 events x Avg NZ$2,000 (GBP£978/US$1204) = NZ$36,000 (GBP£17,605/US$21,677) less the cost of the goods and the cost to attend the events which equalled around a third of total sales, the profit was around NZ$24,000 (GBP£11,737/US$14,451). This didn't

include selling from our shop or on the internet. This again proved to be an excellent side income.

This business did very well for us and we only sold it to be able to focus more fully on other areas of our life. Interestingly, the lady who brought our stock, brought it to create an 'add on' so she could sell horse themed giftware at her riding school.

Pro's

- This is something you can easily 'Add on' to what you are already doing especially if you have a facility that people already come to – when we sold the business it was brought by a riding school that wanted to add this option onto what they were already doing
- For the time invested it is a great little income earner
- You get to spend time at horse shows which is a heap of fun
- You get access to some pretty cool horsey giftware
- This is something you can work around your other commitments

Con's

- You need some capital ($$$) to be able to get started on this option – we started with around NZ$10,000 (GBP£5,000/US$6,000)
- You need to be happy selling – this is a skill you can learn, but if you are good with people it is easy to do
- At some events you won't make money, that does happen but thankfully, that doesn't happen very often but it does allow you to learn which types of events are the best events to attend to sell what you have (if you are selling at events)
- You have to back yourself when purchasing the stock you are going to sell. This can be a bit daunting initially as not everything you like sells, but it I found it didn't take long to

figure out what people wanted to purchase and what they didn't want to purchase

WHAT YOU NEED TO GET STARTED AND BE ABLE TO DO THIS

You will need some initial capital ($$$) to be able to begin this option. What was good, was that even though we invested NZ$10,000 (GBP£5,000/US$6,000) in this to get it started we knew we had the goods to sell if we decided this option wasn't for us so either way we knew we weren't going to lose money.

You will need to find suppliers/wholesales who you can purchase from and meet their requirements to be able to purchase from them. In New Zealand that meant we had to have a Goods and Service Tax number/be an established business, which we already were. You may need to do that in your country.

If you are going to sell at events, you will need to find them and establish what you need to do to get booked in to be able to sell there. We had to purchase a couple of gazebos to run our stall out of.

If you are going to run this from your existing property you will need to establish where and how that will work. We also ended up getting a EFTPOS machine to be able to take payments. There are lots of options for this which you will need to investigate in your country. In New Zealand this required me to have a Business bank account which is different from a personal bank account. You may decide initially to work on a cash basis and then you don't have to worry about that.

Setting up to sell on the internet is remarkable easy. You can create an eCommerce website super easily now days. I did it in no time at all and was able to start selling from my website in a matter of hours. You can also sell on any online sales platform like eBay or Trademe.

Make sure you have a the correct insurance to undertake this type of activity. I had to get extra insurance to cover the goods I had for sale in case of a fire or disaster, you may need to do this as well.

Selling Specialised Equestrian Equipment

WHAT IS IT?
This is where you sell either new or second-hand horse related or equestrian equipment. This differs from a regular saddlery in that you do not try and sell a large range of horse related equipment, rather that you sell specific equipment for a particular breed or equestrian discipline. I have done this successfully and also seen it work for a number of friends.

I imported and sold genuine Parelli Equipment as well as a number of other tools used for training horses. I also have a number of friends who have started up small businesses selling a specific types of equipment. One friend sold equipment specifically used for Endurance riding including special stirrups, saddle blankets and horse heart rate monitors. Another sold equipment specifically used for Arabian horse showing. Everything from special shampoos, show bridles and grooming equipment. In each case, we identified equipment that wasn't easily obtainable, found it, purchased a small amount at a wholesale price, imported it (in my case), and then advertised and sold the equipment for a profit. In my friends cases they increased the range of equipment that they sold and both did extremely well out of it.

Where and how this equipment is sold depends on what works for you. I sold the equipment I had available for sale directly to my students. My friends, both sold theirs online via websites they built themselves as well as taking their products along to their relevant events including the Arabian National Championships and the National Endurance Championships.

POTENTIAL INCOME
The income potential for this option varies greatly depending on how much equipment you have available for sale, what sort of equipment you are selling and where and how you decide to sell it. In my case as I

was primarily selling to my students when they needed extra equipment. I earned around NZ$200 (GBP£97/US$120) per month. My friends made between NZ$500-$5,000 (GBP£244-£2,445/US$300-$3,010) per event.

Pro's
- This option can be worked around any other services you offer/it is very flexible
- If you sell this equipment on the internet, you can do this in the evenings
- This allows you to have access to great equipment at wholesale prices
- This option often helps advertise any other services you are offering because when customers come to you for the equipment, they are often interested to know what else you do
- If you sell at events, this is a great way to spend time at some of your favourite events without necessarily having to compete yourself

Con's
- You have to have enough money to initially invest to purchase the equipment at the outset
- If you are extremely successful at this, this can become very time consuming although you can sell the business and make yet more profit
- You can find the equipment you purchase to sell, doesn't sell

What you need to get started and be able to do this
First you need to find something/some equipment you think will sell. A great way to establish this, is to as they say 'scratch your own itch'. This means find something that you want to purchase, that you find difficult to buy and that is generally a great place to start.

I have found when trying to find the wholesaler of any goods I am looking to source, that the internet is a great place to start looking. Contacting different suppliers and asking if they sell what you are looking for is also a great place to start. You will then need to find out what they need from you in order to be able to supply you with the goods at wholesale. In most cases you will need to open an account with them. I have also found that many companies will start by only supplying you with the goods, when you pay up front for them i.e before they supply them to you. This happens a lot with new customers. After a while they generally allow you to pay the month following the order being delivered.

You will need to establish how you intend to advertise and sell the goods. You may need to set up a website shop or are you going to sell directly at events. Selling on online sales websites such as eBay are a good place to start.

Advertising your goods on any social media sites dedicated to the discipline or breed you are aiming at is also a good place to start.

Make sure you have insurance to cover the goods you have on hand. I had to get special insurance to cover this. My insurance broker was very helpful when it came to organising this.

Show Preparation/Thoroughbred (TB) Yearling Sales Prep

WHAT IS IT?
Although Show Preparation and TB Yearling Sales Prep are not the same thing, they do require similar skills.

Show Preparation is talking about breed preparing breed specific horses for breed specific shows. Thoroughbred Yearling Sales Prep is referring to preparing TB yearlings for the yearling sales. Although this doesn't apply to some countries, it does apply to many.

In both cases what you need to do is take horses and in between 4-12 weeks depending on what you are preparing them for, feed, condition, exercise and educate them, so they not only look outstanding but also understand what their job when they are shown either at their breed specific show or at the yearling sales. Quite a few TB breeders offer Yearling prep, but I have known a number of individuals who have set themselves up doing this and achieved considerable success.

POTENTIAL INCOME
How much you can earn from this is dependant on how many horses you can prepare and how many you can get to prepare.

Prices for this range from NZ$150 (GBP£73/US$90) week plus feed upwards for breed specific show preparation. And the information I have been able to obtain on TB yearling sales preparation ranges from NZ$20 (GBP£10/US$12) day for approx. 60 days (Total of NZ$1,200 (GBP£586/US$722)) up to NZ$60 (GBP£30/US$36) per day for 70 days (NZ$4,200 (GBP£2,045/US$2,5290)) per horse. With TB yearling sales preparation there is a significant focus on fitness not just conditioning, so this is something you would need to take into consideration if you were interested in this option.

Pro's
- This tends to be easier work that some of the other options outlined in this book
- Depending on how many horses you take on, you can make a reasonable amount of money doing this
- The sales and shows happen at the same time each year, so it is easy to plan other work around this
- I have not found many people that offer breed specific show preparation so there is definitely an opportunity for this

Con's
- You have to do this rain, hail or snow as there is a deadline that doesn't move because the horse you are preparing doesn't look its best
- Getting clients can take a while as people want to see the results of your work, but you can't get results until you get work so sometimes this can be a difficult to overcome/conundrum
- You need to have good facilities including stables to be able to offer this service because in order to get a horse fit that is not broken in requires a good surface on which to work and you cannot have horses getting injured for obvious reasons

What you need to get started and be able to do this
You will need to either to or know how to condition/show prep a horse – you can a learn a lot about this on the internet or reading books if you don't already know. You can also take lessons from someone who is already doing this.

Excellent facilities for reasons already stated as well as enough time to work the number of horses you want to take.

You will need a contract with the horse owner similar to the breaking in contract stating what they will pay for and when.

You will need to advertise in places where the customers you are after will read e.g. Breed specific publications or social media channels and the same for yearling sales prep. A great website helps with this.

Teaching a Specific Skill to a Horse

WHAT IS IT?
Normally this involves you taking a horse(s) and teaching them a specific skill e.g. to tie up happily or to trailer load or be caught willingly. This differs from Foundation training in that Foundation training generally works on producing an all around horse where as this option focuses on teaching one or two specific skills. Sometimes this is done onsite at the owners property but that restricts your flexibility and ability to work on the horse when it suits you.

POTENTIAL INCOME
Generally trainers have a set fee for this e.g. NZ$300 - NZ$1,000 (GBP£146-£489/US$180-$602) to teach it to tie up or trailer load or be washed or whichever specific skill the owner wants addressed. Generally trainers indicate how long they expect it to take or how long they expect to have the horse for e.g. 1-4 weeks.
How much you can make again depends on how many clients you can find that want their horse taught the specific skill you can teach and how much time each day, you have available that you can dedicate to teaching a horse(s).

PRO'S
- This work can be very flexible – you can generally organise it around anything else you are doing
- This is a great way to spend time around horses
- This is a great to learn lots of new skills – especially when you encounter a horse that doesn't respond to your solution
- This is a great way to get clients – I have had a number of people who have come to me for this service and ended up coming to clinics I run or take individual lessons from me
- You will get to teach a lot of different horses and ponies

Con's
- It can take a while to build up a client base who want this service
- Some horses won't respond to your way of teaching/fixing the problem and some horses will require a lot more time than you expect or plan for
- Some horses can be extremely difficult and even dangerous – you have to be prepared to walk away and give the owner back their money as getting injured would mean you won't be able to work

What You Need to Get Started and Be Able to Do This

You have to be able to teach the skills you are going to offer e.g. to tie up, trailer load or be caught.

The good thing about this is you can study so many different options on the internet these days to learn.

If you have the skills to do this, next you need to find clients. Again spreading the word via social media is a great option or getting in contact with local riding groups and offering to do a free demonstration what you can teach is great option.

You also need to make sure you have got the right insurance to cover you should something go wrong and you or the horse get injured.

Thoroughbred Racehorse Breeding

WHAT IS IT?
This is where you purchase a registered Thoroughbred mare, breed her to a registered thoroughbred stallion, or purchase a registered thoroughbred mare already in foal and then produce the foal and then when the foal is weaned, sell it. There are many people who do this all over the world. As so few racehorses actually make good racehorses, there is always a demand for more 'potential' winning race horses. Being able to handle and produce great looking young horses is a key to success with this option.

In the last weanling sale held at Karaka which is New Zealand's premier Thoroughbred selling facility, 105 weanlings sold for an aggregate of NZ$3,486,000 (GBP£1,704,834/US$2,099,094). The average was NZ$33,200 (GBP£16,236/US$19,991), while the median was NZ$16,000 (GBP£7,824/US$9,634) and the clearance rate closed at 88%. That means 88% of the weanlings offered were sold. And as you can place a reserve on your weanling prior to it selling, one would expect that in most cases these horses made their owners some profit.

POTENTIAL INCOME
The income potential for this option varies greatly depending on how much money you have to invest on the initial mare you purchase, as well as how much money you have to invest in the stallion you choose to cover your mare. Thoroughbred Stallion service fees range from hundreds of dollars through to millions of dollars. Or if you purchase a mare in foal, then the cost of the stud fee is included in the cost of mare, so this may be a better option. On top of the cost of the mare, is the service fee and any related expenses incurred while the mare is at stud being bred. There is also the cost of feeding and caring for the mare and ultimately preparing the weanling for sale. It costs approximately NZ$1,000 (GBP£489/US$602) to care for a horse per year if you own your own land. If you pay up to NZ$4,000

(GBP£1,956/US$2,408) for a broodmare already in foal, this is a total cost of NZ$5,000 (GBP£2,445/US$3,010). Add to this the cost of listing your weanling for sale. If you use the likes of Gavelhouse to sell your weanling, it costs NZ$320 (GBP£156/US$192) to list the weanling and then they take 5% of the sale price. If you sell your weanling for the medium sale price of NZ$16,000 (GBP£7,824/US$9,634) (as documented above) that is a total cost of NZ$320 (GBP£156/US$192) listing fee + NZ$800 (GBP£391/US$481) commission = NZ$1,120 (GBP£545/US$674) + costs of purchasing and caring for your mare for a year NZ$5,000 (GBP£2,445/US$3,010) = NZ$6,120 (GBP£2,993/US$3,685) total cost. If you get the medium price for your weanling foal of NZ$16,000 (GBP£7,824/US$9,634) that is nearly a NZ$10,000 (GBP£4,890/US$6,021) profit and you still have the mare to breed again or sell.

These are rough estimates, but they give you a reasonable indication of what is possible. It is possible to make a lot more money from each foal than this, and it is also possible to make a lot less.

Two Examples of in foal broodmares available for sale, on the Thoroughbred horse auction currently being ran by Gavelhouse.com as I write this book. The reserve price for each of these mares was NZ$500 (GBP£244/US$310). Their actual sale price is shown at the end of each example.

Example One - Danzero mare offered as an unreserved in foal breeding proposition. prolific producer of colts ,She has had 8 foals for 7 colts in a row. She leaves good strong types as you can see by the photo of her chestnut yearling colt by Ribchester now 3 years old retained by Gary who he rates highly. Yearlings have sold up to NZ$200,000 (GBP£97,810/US$120,430) and trial horses sold to HK. In foal to the very well Breed Son of Zabeel, The Good Looking Boy Ocean Emperor. Ocean Emperor leaves great types with his kind nature. He has had weanlings and yearlings sell for up to NZ$75,000 (GBP£36,678/US$45,161). Standing for NZ$11,500

(GBP£5,500/US$6,800). This mare sold for NZ$2,000 (GBP£978/US$1,204).

Example Two - Classy Lane A daughter of the renowned Pentire, who is now established as a successful broodmare sire. Classy Lane was lightly raced and was retired due to a recurring injury issue. She showed great promise, winning at her second start and running a number of placings. Classy Lane's first five dams were all multiple winners, with her immediate dam, High Vibes, being bred from the sire line of Star Kingdom which has nicked very well with Pentire. Classy Lane is in foal to Zed and due to foal in November. The Zed / Pentire mating has proven itself to be a successful and sought after cross, producing the likes of Jack's Star and Anniestar (dam of current Nz/Aus G1 performer Charm's Star). She is an attractive mare, standing at approximately 15.3 hands and easy to do anything with. She currently is being treated for rain scald although this is expected to resolve quickly. This mare sold for NZ$700 (GBP£342/US$421).

Pro's

- This is a great way to spend heaps of time working with and caring for horses
- This is a great way to improve your young horse handling skills
- This is a learn about how to prepare young horses for sale
- This can be a great income earner

Con's

- Some broodmares can be difficult particularly when they have a foal – good horsemanship skills can help with this
- You need to have the right facilities to work with young horses – facilities that allow you to work with them and care for them in an environment where they cannot hurt themselves
- If the foal has a confirmational defect, gets injured or dies you don't make any money

- You need to have a paddock close to your house where you can foal the mare. A foaling alarm also helps with this
- If the mare loses the foal for any reason, you don't make any money
- If the mare or foal get injured, you will be up for vet bills that come off the cost of what you were potentially going to make

WHAT YOU NEED TO GET STARTED AND BE ABLE TO DO THIS

You will need to learn a bit about Thoroughbred Horse pedigrees so you can understand the breeding lines you are buying. A little bit of research can help immensely with this. I spend some time researching pedigrees and watched the sales to see what was selling for what money and what was popular currently which also helps you to make a good decision when purchasing your broodmare.

You need to have the knowledge, experience and facilities to foal the mare. This doesn't always go as it should so it pays to be well researched in advance. You need to have the skills to care for and wean a foal and well as the ability to turn the weanling out for sale. Again these skills can be learnt.

You need to have suitable facilities to be able to train the weanling to lead, tie up, wear a rug, have its feet done and teach it to be bathed. Basically teaching it the basics of how to be a horse living in a humans world.

You need only google search Thoroughbred sales in your country, to find out where and how Thoroughbreds are sold in your country. Do some research on this to find out where and how they are sold and what sort of money is being paid for Thoroughbred broodmares and weanlings in your country.

Transporting Horses

WHAT IS IT?
This is where you are paid to transport horses from one place to another. In New Zealand this is not a regulated activity which means anyone can do it. Here in New Zealand we have big Corporate compies that run fleets of horse trucks all around the country every day transporting horses from one of New Zealand to the other. As well as this we have private individuals who transport horses in their purpose built horse floats locally and nationally.

There are always lots of opportunities for horse transporters as there are always horses being brought and sold and needing to be shifted all over the countryside.

POTENTIAL INCOME
The income potential for this varies greatly as it depends on what sort of transportation you have available (10 space Horse Truck or 3 space Horse trailer/float). The 10 space horse truck is hugely profitable if you can run it full all the time, but if you can't then the 3 horse trailer running full is a much better proposition.

To transport a horse from Auckland which is in the North Island of New Zealand to Christchurch which is in the South Island can cost upwards of NZ$1,100 (GBP£537/US$662) for one horse. They require overnight accommodation half way as it is too far to travel in one trip and they need to travel across the Cook Straight on a Ferry which adds another 4+ hours to the journey. The trucks carry 6-9 horses which means each trip is grossing NZ$6,600-$9,900 (GBP£3,227-£4,841/US$3,974-$5,961). Off this cost comes the cost of the fuel, the wear and tear on the truck, the drivers salary, the cost of the office staff who do the accounts and the cost of the ferry but this still leaves makes this a good income earner.

The private individuals who are doing this have lower overheads as they don't need to employ staff to answer the phones or process the accounts, they can do that themselves but they also generally have smaller trucks or horse floats/trailers so can't take as many horses any given time. I know a number of people who have started doing this because it is such a good income earner. One individual would also transport dogs and other animals in the front of his horse trailer to make each journey more cost effective.

Pro's

- This is a great way to improve your horsemanship because you get the opportunity to load lots of horses onto your truck or trailer. Nothing improves horsemanship quicker than learning how to load a horse onto a horse truck or trailer when it is not keen to go in.
- You get to spend heaps of time working with and caring for lots of different horses
- This can be a great income earner

Con's

- Some horses can be very difficult to load onto a horse truck or trailer – I know the drivers who do this become very good at figuring out what option will work best for what horse
- You can get injured dealing with horses that have little or no handling or simply do not know how to respond when asked to lead or keep out of your personal space. You cannot earn any money if you are injured ☹
- Some horses can cause considerable damage to your horse truck/trailer
- Some horses can get injured while travelling if they are very claustrophobic – you need to ensure you have the correct insurances to cover this eventuality
- You need to ensure the horses travel is paid for in advance to ensure you get paid as some people do not pay their bills

WHAT YOU NEED TO GET STARTED AND BE ABLE TO DO THIS

You will need a suitable horse truck or trailer/float suitable for transporting horses who are seasoned travellers and those that are not and who really do not want to be locked in a moving horse truck/trailer.

You will need to ensure you have the correct insurance to cover you for all eventualities included driver accidents or accidents involving loading, unloading or travelling the horses.

For this type of service I would definitely set up a website. You can have someone do this for you or you can do it yourself. There are lots of website building tools that can help you with this.

Advertising on local social media is generally enough to get this type of business up and running.

Vet Assistant at an Equine Hospital

WHAT IS IT?
Specialist Equine hospitals have increased in recent years. This is because horses have become increasingly popular over the last 20 years and many vets only want to work with small animals so the need for specialist equine focused vets has increased.

To work at an Equine Hospital you do not necessarily need to be a qualified vet or vet nurse. These hospitals need a host of other staff including stable work staff and vet assistants who help hold, catch and take care of the horses that come into the hospital. One local Equine hospital has approximately 75 staff, with only 20 of those being qualified veterinaries so there are lots of different opportunities to work at these establishments with horses. The key to being able to get one of these roles is to have good horse handling skills.

POTENTIAL INCOME
The gross annual salary of an entry level Vet Assistant in New Zealand is NZ$44,095 (GBP£21,547/US$26,551) (2022). Salaries appear to be similar in other parts of the world.

PRO'S
- You get to work with a huge range of horses and people
- You get to help a lot of horses
- You will learn a lot about caring for horses and what can be done to help them with different illnesses and injuries

CON'S
- Some horses can be very difficult to work with especially when they are injured - good horsemanship skills can really you with help – you can do courses on this or spend time with someone experienced

- Getting the initial skills required to get the job may take some time and require working for someone experienced with training or handling horses prior be able to get one of these roles

WHAT YOU NEED TO GET STARTED AND BE ABLE TO DO THIS

You will need good horsemanship/horse handling skills to be able to get one of these roles. I have covered this above. Another potential option is to offer to volunteer at these types of establishment initially to gain some skills that you can then put on your CV. Next you need to put a CV together outlining your skills. There are lots of tools on the Internet that can help you with this. Search out and apply for roles. If it were me looking for one of these roles, I would physically take my CV into each place and drop it off, saying what you are looking for. Prospective employers often like people who take initiative.

Virtual Lessons

WHAT IS IT?
Again these have become popular since the Pandemic. A virtual lesson is where you give a lesson to someone located at a completely different location and sometimes country from where you.
There are several ways to do this:
1. You do this either by simply talking a person through what they need to do via the phone or an internet webinar
2. Students can send you videos of themselves and then you talk them person through what they need to do to improve
3. Someone or something (Like a PIVO) can video the student real time while you provide feedback.

Different instructors have different preferences. I have a number of groups of students that get together on a regular basis (fortnightly) where we talk through what they have been doing with their horses, any problems they have got and what to focus on next. This works extremely well as it keeps the students accountable and it also provides them with a portal/opportunity to have the questions or issues resolved without actually having to travel to me with their horse for a lesson.

POTENTIAL INCOME
One instructor I had a virtual lesson with charges US$125 (GBP£100/NZ$207) per hour. He was excellent. We did a zoom (Online) meeting and a covered all my questions in under an hour. He gives virtual lessons as well as in person lessons, clinics, camps and takes horses for training.

I charge NZ$100 (GBP£48/US$60) per hour. Sometimes I do 3-4 virtual lessons a week and sometimes less. Again this is something I do as well as a number of other options in this book.

If you did 5 virtual lessons a week and charge NZ$100 (GBP£48/US$60) per lesson, that's NZ$500 (GBP£244/US$300) a week.

PRO'S
- There is lots of flexibility on when and how you can do this
- You are not limited to only the students that can bring their horses to you
- There is a myriad of ways you can do the virtual lessons – by phone, by webinars, by zoom calls etc

CON'S
- Getting students/customers to sign up for this/to see the value in this type of teaching can initially be difficult but is definitely possible as I have found

WHAT YOU NEED TO GET STARTED AND BE ABLE TO DO THIS

You will need students who want what you teach.

You need to advertise what you can do for them. You can deliver these lessons using any of the aforementioned delivery styles. Zoom is free and easy to use, so certainly worth investigating.

This is a great option especially if you already teach riding or horsemanship in person.

Working on a Yard/Stable Groom

WHAT IS IT?
There are many jobs available working on Yards. A Yard is the name given to the location/facility where trainers base themselves to train their horses. I know of positions on ranches in the USA where the owners are looking for someone to take care of their 18 various horses. I know of a huntsman who is runs a local hunt who has been looking for someone to work for him, caring for and exercising his horses as they require a high level of fitness. He is the loveliest man and a great teacher. I know of a Natural Horseman who is always looking for working students to muck out, care for and help him train horses. I have known a number of dressage riders looking for grooms to muck out, care for and help them work their horses. I know a stud that has 38 horses including 6 stallions that has been looking for someone to come and care for and train their horses for the last 6 months and has not been able to find someone with the skills to work with stallions as those skills are not easy to come.

This option of working or a yard or as a groom is very varied depending on what discipline you are interested in and your willingness to work. Working with horses in a yard or as a groom can be very physically demanding but it can also be an incredible way to learn a lot.

Having a heavy traffic license so you can drive a horse truck/lorry is definitely an advantage.

POTENTIAL INCOME
How much you can earn from this is dependant on your level of skill and also what you are prepared to do.

I have been quoted NZ$100 (GBP£48/US$60) week including food and board up to US$50,000 (GBP£24,452/NZ$83,035) per year and I suspect for some very experienced this would be higher. Many Yard/groom positions come with accommodation and food.

A good place to start looking is the website www.yardandgroom.com.

Pro's
- You get paid to work with horses all day everyday!
- You often get to learn from someone more experienced than you
- You often get to ride some incredible horses that you would not normally have access to

Con's
- The work can be very physically hard and if you do not want to pick up horse manure, then this option is not for you
- There can be limited days off during the competitions season if you are working for a competition yard
- The pay can be low when you are first starting out
- You generally have to do the work no one else wants to do

What you need to get started and be able to do this

The biggest thing about this, is the willingness to work hard day in day out (did I say that already?!?!). If you like to look at your cell phone, then this option is definitely not for you. You have to be prepared work and work and work.

Often for type of work you don't need too many skills except for a willingness to learn. More skills are required, the more specialised you get, but often the trainers are willing to take someone with less skills if you have a positive attitude and a willingness to work hard.

If you Google the following words 'yard', 'groom' and horses in any app that advertises jobs you will find these types of jobs.

Young Horse Nursery

WHAT IS IT?
This option differs from the 'General Horse Grazing/Boarding/Livery Services' option in that normally the horses involved in this option are turned out in groups with other horses of similar age and personality in larger paddocks and for a longer periods of time/up to years. You as the facility owner look after them and the owner only sees these horses occasionally, if at all.

This option has come about because many people want their young horses to grow up in a herd with lots of space to move and develop their bones and muscles, but don't usually have the time or the space to accommodate this themselves.

Young Horse Nurseries have become more popular in recent times as horse owners have become more aware of the importance of the early years of development of a horse, to its long term performance abilities.

POTENTIAL INCOME
How much you can earn for this depends on how much space you have available and how many horses you have the time to take care of. Because these horses are turned out (not in work), there tends to be a lot less work (your time) involved. Of course if a horse gets injured or requires special care, that is not necessarily the case.

Note:- I have worked these possible incomes on 10 horses. Many of the facilities I found who offer this service, accommodate considerably more than 10 horses, but this at least gives you an idea of what is possible.

Example One – 200 acres of excellent pastures with gentle hills and nice atmosphere. Hay fed in winter, large paddocks that are not overstocked with experienced handles. Prices NZ$: Weanlings/Yearlings - hard fed - NZ$25 (GBP£12/US$15) per day/ Winter rate 1 June to 30 September NZ$28 (GBP£14/US$17) per day. Total per year for 10 young horses = 10 x NZ$25 (GBP£12/US$15) day x 365 = NZ$91,250 (GBP£44,000/US$54,000)

Example Two – pastures range in size from five to 20 acres, varying terrain with trees. Horses are in small herds. Prices start from NZ$57 (GBP£28/US$34) per week (includes hay as needed, hoof care, worming, and photo updates). Horses are checked daily. Total per year for 10 horses = 10 x NZ$57 (GBP£28/US$34) x 52 = NZ$29,640 (GBP£14,500/US$17,500).

PRO'S

- As the horses are generally turned out (in the pasture all the time), they tend to require less work than a full service Liberty stable where the horses are often stabled and then turned out for a portion of the day – generally daily checking and in winter the feeding of hay or supplemental feed is all that is required
- If you already have the space and facilities, this can be a simple, reasonably easy money making option where you get to work and interact with lots of horses
- This is a great way to meet lots of people and lots of different horses

CON'S

- Sometimes owners don't pay their bill, so you need to have strategies in place to ensure you get paid. These could include legal contracts and/or written agreement with the owners prior to accepting their horses
- If a horse you have grazing at your property gets injured, you will need to tend to it and also make sure you have the correct liability and insurances to cover yourself for this eventuality

- Horse owners wanting to visit their horses at inconvenient times of the day or weekend – you can stipulate when they can visit in the contract to alleviate issues surrounding this
- Some horses can be difficult to catch and deal with especially if they get injured and require attention from a vet – good horsemanship skills can help immensely with this

WHAT YOU NEED TO GET STARTED AND BE ABLE TO DO THIS

You will need a boarding contact/agreement. I decided not to include a sample boarding contact in this book because every country around the world has different legal requirements. If you do a Google search on horse boarding or grazing for horses in your country, you will be able to find numerous examples of boarding contracts that you can use as a starting point. Another option is to seek the advice of a lawyer on this. They can make sure you are covered legally as well as ensuring you are in a position to be able to collect any unpaid fees.

If you offer these services, it could be worth creating a website and advertising this. You can also advertise on any local equestrian social media sites to get your name out there. You can also email local studs directly advising you offer this service. Word of mouth normally takes over after a period of time.

Ensure you have the necessary insurances as well as being very clear about what you will and will not do for the horses in your care.